A LIFE

WITHOUT LIMITS

Sir Bert Massie CBE DL

Disability Rights Activist and Advocate

Mereo Books

1A The Wool Market Dyer Street Cirencester Gloucestershire GL7 2PR
An imprint of Memoirs Books Ltd. www.mereobooks.com

A Life Without Limits: 978-1-86151-905-4

First published in Great Britain in 2019
by Mereo Books, an imprint of Memoirs Books Ltd.

Copyright ©2019

The address for Memoirs Books Ltd. can be
found at www.mereobooks.com

Memoirs Books Ltd. Reg. No. 7834348

Typeset in 12.5/21pt Helvetica
by Wiltshire Associates Ltd.
Printed and bound in Great Britain by Biddles Books

Preface

In writing this memoir I have two objectives. The first is to give an account of my personal history as somebody who became disabled at the age of three months soon after the end of World War II and therefore grew up with the development of the welfare state and the birth of disability rights. Each person's journey will be different, but I believe many of the obstacles I faced, as well as the support and encouragement I received, will be familiar to many disabled people.

My journey started in a large working-class family living in a provincial northern city. It has finished with a number of the glittering prizes of middle-class respectability, although my roots remain in that working-class background. It was an unusual journey and perhaps worth recording.

Disability and its consequences have been a large part of my life, as have been the disability organisations that have helped and supported me. I refer freely to my impairment of polio, and some disabled people will criticise me for this as they believe we are impaired, but disability is caused by society. I will explain this debate later, but it was not current for the first half of my life. As I grew up I was very much aware I was one of the polio group and was treated accordingly. My experience was different from that of a blind person or someone with a different impairment.

The other purpose, and the more important one, is to record the development of disability rights in the UK and sometimes further afield. This is not a full history of disability, disabled people or even disability rights. I have sought to record the developments in which I was personally involved and therefore of which I can offer some insight into how policy was developed and implemented. In doing so I am conscious that I was never the single person who devised or implemented major policy developments. It was always a collaborative process. It was my honour to work with so many committed and wonderful people, many of whom were disabled, although equally many were not. Teamwork has been at the heart of everything.

Inevitably the two broad themes of my life are intertwined and I have made no attempt to separate them, as it would be impossible to do so. Had I not been disabled, my life would have taken a different course.

Looking back on my career, I can reflect on the many significant improvements in support for disabled people. For example, the Disablement Income Group led the battle for financial support for disabled people during the 1960s and 1970s. They presented strong coherent arguments on why change was needed. In contrast, from the late 1990s onwards there has been a consistent determination by government to reduce disability benefits, and as a consequence disabled people are returning to the poverty we faced in the 1950s.

There needs to be a clearer appreciation of why the benefit system evolved the way it did. Much of the same can be said of policy relating to the mobility of disabled people and of housing. The 1970s saw a renaissance of welfare and social care support for disabled people, but the late 1980s saw moves to reverse this progress. Apart from those with the highest needs, most of the support has been scrapped because it is seen as too expensive. It is, I think, worth recording what was achieved, so we can set our ambitions towards a better future.

People become disabled through a range of factors, and as a young man I concentrated my efforts on campaigning on issues that affected me personally. This memoir is therefore biased. It was much later in my career that blind people, deaf people and others began to assert themselves. People with mental health issues were hidden away in institutions. People with learning disabilities formed their own organisations to ensure their voice was heard. There are books waiting to be written about the struggle for rights that all these groups experienced. That is not the aim of this memoir. If I was not involved in some way, I deal with such issues only in passing.

However, I think we are missing accounts of individuals who were involved in some of the battles and witnessed others first-hand. To ensure that disabled people enjoy human and civil rights was a mammoth task that involved tens of thousands of disabled people as well as our allies. If we allow these to be unpicked, it could be at least a generation or two before they can be recreated. That is the task that lies before disabled activists today, and it is an uphill task, because so many of the support mechanisms, such as local authority financial backing for organisations for disabled people, have disappeared. It is also important that disabled people ensure politicians understand that ideological policies frequently have a negative impact on the independence of disabled people.

So often I have witnessed ideology eclipse rational thinking and seen the horrid consequences that have made life more difficult for disabled people. If nothing else, I hope this memoir will remind people of the value of what has been achieved.

This memoir is therefore inevitably the partial one-sided view of one individual, but I hope that enhances rather than diminishes it.

Footnote, by Lady Massie
My husband asked towards the end of his life that his memoir should acknowledge the part played by two

former colleagues, Ann Frye and Bob Niven, in helping to complete the text (especially chapter 12) and bring it to publication. I was, and remain, very grateful to them.

For Maureen

CONTENTS

Foreword, by Lord Blunkett

Foreword

By Lord Blunkett of Brightside and Hillsborough

Bert's story, told in this memoir, is an extraordinary journey of determination, resilience and courage combined with great intelligence and an ever-present sense of humour.

Bert rose to national prominence and recognition as a disability campaigner and social reformer, but he never forgot his Liverpool roots or his childhood struggles with disability and poverty. He made an enormous contribution, not just to disability rights but actually to ensuring that the voice of people with disabilities was heard in ways that it hadn't been before.

I had the greatest respect for Bert throughout his career. It was at the Royal Association for Disability & Rehabilitation (RADAR) that he first really came into his own at national level. RADAR was a great name because it was about questioning the environment, it was about finding out where the dangers were, it was about steering a course towards disability rights. Bert at RADAR was a phenomenon in himself.

When I asked Bert to chair the Disability Rights Commission and he enthusiastically accepted, his negotiating skills were absolutely fundamental. People were arguing on the head of a pin. He had to do all the hard graft behind the scenes of getting people to work together.

The one thing that should light a candle and keep us all going is the memory of Bert's expertise and his excellent way of persuading people, with his inimitable wit and humour, to do things that they didn't want to do, and also his tenacity in keeping going over those years.

Bert's lasting legacy is a transformation in the rights of people with disabilities, in legislation, policy and practice.

We all owe Bert a huge debt of gratitude and we need to ensure that his spirit lives on.

David Blunkett

Chapter 1

Polio Strikes

It was the day that changed my life and dramatically set it on a course that could not have been anticipated, but I have no memory of it; I was only three months old, after all. Such images as I have are drawn from the memories of others and, like all memories, they might have been affected by the fog and blurred vision of the passing years. The same picture is seen differently from another angle and through another's eyes. But these borrowed memories are all I have of that day. I was given a starring role, but remained ignorant of the script.

My nineteen-year old mother was the first to spot

the change. Something was wrong. The infant in her arms was listless and vomiting up his food. His eyes were unfocused, his temperature rising. His body lacked its usual vitality and strength. It was floppy, the left arm immobile, the right one weak, and both legs lay useless. She was an experienced mother with a one-year-old daughter, but this was something she had not witnessed before. I was a tiny infant, and my behaviour and condition were frightening.

Mum and Dad were living with Dad's parents in a small terraced house in Roxburgh Street in north Liverpool. In seeking help, Mum did not turn to her in-laws but to her own mother, who lived a few miles away. My Grandma Roberts was a tough, resourceful woman. She had remained in Liverpool during the worst the Luftwaffe could throw at the city and, while her husband sailed on the Atlantic convoys bringing food, materials and weapons from the United States, she had raised their four children. My mother had told her how worried she was that I had a fever and was listless. The energy in her three-month-old baby had disappeared. Grandma knew the signs. Speed was essential. There was no time to call an ambulance, and a taxi would have meant spending the rent money. Few people owned telephones in 1949 and no neighbour was sufficiently wealthy to own a car.

So Grandma grabbed me and carried me to the busy Stanley Road, with its constant flow of lorries and carts servicing Liverpool's still bustling docks that lined the banks of the River Mersey. Gran stepped into the road in front of a lorry, whose driver had little choice but to apply his brakes. It would take a man of great courage to refuse an instruction from my formidable Gran. She ordered the driver to take her and me to Myrtle Street Hospital. Having agreed, his immediate problem was getting Gran into the high and inaccessible cab of his lorry, which was larger than the average house. He got out and while Gran pulled herself into the cab he applied pressure to her bottom and eased her in. Such is the family story.

Mum was left behind to look after my sister Joan, who was just over a year old. We drove from Stanley Road to the city centre until we reached Myrtle Street Children's Hospital, which, like many Victorian hospitals, has since been demolished. It has been replaced by Myrtle Street Community College and Arts Centre, where many years later my brother Wayne would work as a caretaker. And so I began a lifelong association with the medical profession, which to this day has left me with a deep and abiding suspicion of many, but happily not all, doctors.

In 1949 my mother was a young woman, already married with two kids, and like a lot of young people of the time she was keen to look her best. Despite the poverty of the time, this she managed to do by making clothes last and by placing cardboard in worn-out shoes to give them extra life. She was attractive and had red hair which when caught by the sun was rich in autumn shades, from warm copper to burnished gold. She had an elegance that would have given many an actress a run for their money. While rearing two babies, for three hours every night she worked at Jacobs' biscuit factory. During the day Dad worked as a carter around the docks, with his cart being drawn by a horse.

Before she was old enough to vote, Mum already had considerable responsibilities. She had given birth to my sister Joan a year earlier and had not started her married life in the best of circumstances. She was living in the home of her in-laws, Herbert and Eva Massie, a three-up three-down terraced house. Living with in-laws was quite usual then because of the acute shortage of housing. Liverpool was a major port and had been essential to the war effort. In that sense it was a legitimate target for the German bombers. They aimed for the Liverpool docks and their cargo ships. The bombs that missed their targets flattened houses in the crowded streets near the river. Some people have since argued that the Luftwaffe did Liverpool a favour, because by the liberal and generous use of high explosive, they helped to clear huge areas of slum housing. But it was a dangerous type of demolition, because it cost over 2,000 lives. It was as though Coventry had moved to the banks of the Mersey.

My mother had her opinion of the war. Like many people of her generation, she suffered her share of horror and tragedy. She told me how Grandma had come home one day after seeing a bomb hit a bus packed with people. As the bomb found its mark the bus exploded into a crimson ball, looking like a huge dahlia. Human flesh was sent flying in all directions and as she looked down she saw a head rolling towards her, so freshly parted from its body that blood was still oozing from where the neck had been seconds earlier. The face still had a look of startled terror. It was an image that remained.

She was not the only family member to suffer the privations of war. My Grandad, George Roberts, was a merchant seaman and took part in that vital struggle for our survival which became known as the "Battle of the Atlantic". He was sunk at least once; he was an unwitting victim of what the German U boat crews called their "happy time". They thought they were well on their way to victory. My grandad must have thought so too as he bobbed up and down in the swell. When I knew him he was shaped a bit like a cork and seemingly floated like one. I recall him teaching me to tell the time but he never spoke of the burning ship he had refused to leave until he had rescued several members of the crew, at great risk to himself. I suppose he would have seen it as just another war story among millions.

I had been in hospital six weeks since my ride in the lorry, and still the doctors appeared to have no idea what was wrong with me. Questions were asked of them, but were always met with a vague, uninterested response. An attitude prevailed then with some doctors who seemed to regard working, uneducated people, as little better than peasants who could not be expected to understand the dark arts or the enlightened science of medical practice.

Grandma grew very impatient with this patronising approach and exploded with all the fury of a repressed class which had just struggled through a vicious war and now demanded to be heard. She assailed the German doctor who was in charge of my case, and was eventually given the gloomy news that I had "infantile paralysis". This was the popular name for what became known as "poliomyelitis" or as I came to know it, polio. This was catastrophic news for my family, although I was blissfully unaware of it. However, I must have been made of the same toughness that was typical of the rest of my family. Polio can kill, but mostly it doesn't. It is a short-lived virus, but it leaves its former host with lifelong memories and effects of the visit.

Polio has been around for at least about 3000 years. Caused by a virus that enters the bloodstream and attacks the central nervous system, it affects the nerves that control muscles, and this results in muscle wastage. The term 'poliomyelitis' comes from the Greek "polios" meaning grey and "myelos" meaning matter. The grey matter referred to is found in the spinal cord. When the nerves die the muscles they serve can become weakened. The respiratory muscles in this situation can be especially vulnerable.

Many people would contract the polio virus and only experience mild symptoms. At three months old I knew nothing about what was happening to me. I must have experienced some difficulty in moving about and my mother would have been sensitive to this.

Apart from the emotional shock, it affected my parents in practical ways. They would visit me frequently but could not afford the bus fares, so they had to walk across the city to get to the hospital.

For the rest of her life my mother blamed an infected hypodermic needle that had been used when I had a vaccination. I think she was probably mistaken about this, because in 1949 there was no vaccine to be had for polio. There was a lot of research being done in the USA to try and find a suitable vaccine, but sadly that would take another five years.

The two men who produced the first successful vaccine were to fight each other bitterly and developed a deep hatred for each other. Salk produced the first vaccine using dead polio virus, and this became the first effective defence against polio. Sabin thought it better to use a live virus, as this would provide longer-term protection. However, it was not until the 1960s, that decade which is defined by its music and in which I became a teenager, that polio vaccine was widely used. A full discussion of the development of the polio vaccine is contained in an excellent book by Tony Gould[1].

Myrtle Street had done all they could, but they thought I could not survive outside a hospital. I was transferred to one of Europe's largest children's hospitals, Alder Hey, which just happened to be in Liverpool. Alder Hey started life as a workhouse and was to be found in one of Liverpool's oldest districts, West Derby, which is mentioned in the Doomsday Book of 1086. The Board of the Poor Law Guardians bought it in 1910. At that time it was a luxury mansion, and it was their intention to convert the building into a care home for poor children. When it became a hospital in 1914 Britain was already involved in a war, so it was used to treat the wounded.

Alder Hey was to be my home for the next five years. When children are in the early years of life they expect and receive plenty of love and affection and warm cuddles from their parents. These I received during the strictly limited visiting times when Mum could visit and when I was allowed home

---

1. Gould, Tony. A Summer Plague: Polio and its Survivors, Yale University Press, New Haven & London 1995

on occasional weekends. The prevailing view was that hospital was the best place for me. My earliest memories are of nurses in stiff starched uniforms. Instead of warm human scents I was conscious of the clean cold aroma of ether. Nurses try to do things with you, but mostly the medical regime required them to do things *to* you. I was a small child for some of the time but mostly I was the patient to whom things were done. However, I do not recall this as an unhappy time. Young children are infinitely adaptable and make the best of the situation in which they find themselves.

My world became a long hospital ward with beds arranged in a long row on either side. They were high and designed to enable the nurses to avoid bending too much. Their design was basic. They had grey tubular steel legs and the base was formed by springs attached to the side of the frame to which was attached a metal matrix of diamond-shaped spaces between the steel wire. A thin mattress was placed on top. Whoever designed these beds could never have slept in them.

In addition to the ether, the other all-pervading smell was of polish and cleaning materials. In those days medical and other staff knew the importance of hygiene. The floor was highly polished wood, and was it polished! Several times a day, cleaners with large brushes, dusters and machines with round brushes at their base would ingrain an endless supply of polish into the wood. One advantage of all this labour was that the floor was always clean and, while it was slippery for those walking, it was ideal for children who were unable to walk and who instead moved around at great speed on their bottoms. Being disabled was no reason not to have fun.

Besides, none of us thought of ourselves as disabled. Looking around, the order of the world was clear. Grown-ups could walk and most of the kids couldn't. We would probably walk when we grew up. It really wasn't an issue that worried us.

Constant physiotherapy and the body's own ability to reroute nerves to damaged muscles eventually resulted in useful movement in some of my limbs. None of them ever recovered fully, but some strength returned. I grew from a baby into a toddler who couldn't toddle. I was unable to stand on either leg and both arms were weak, although there was useful strength in my right arm. But this was all the strength I needed to swing underneath the high hospital beds. Indeed, there was so much room under the beds that dens could be created in the mistaken belief that the grown-ups did not know we were there.

These were the days when the medical profession believed that above all crippled children needed fresh air. The poor dears never learned the distinction between air that was fresh and air that was freezing. At the end of the ward there was a veranda, and once

the young patients were deemed strong enough, t
beds were moved there. Any impression that this
was like living in a conservatory should be instantly
squashed. Conservatories are protected by glass,
but all we had were black iron bars to separate us
from the universe. In warm weather this was not too
bad, but Alder Hey knew nothing of the seasons. We
were placed on the veranda regardless of weather.
In the winter the snow would blow through the bars
and land on the bottoms of all the beds. Anxious that
the bedclothes should not get wet, staff would place
rubber sheets across the bottoms of the beds. This
was effective in keeping the snow off the bedclothes,
but it made them so heavy it was difficult to move feet
or legs under the vice-like weight.

Of course, the concern was not just for the bedding.
We kids also needed some protection. A heater
would have been a good idea, but instead we were
given balaclavas to place on our heads and we slept
in these. A jumper over our pyjamas completed our
protection. We looked like members of an infantile
terrorist cell safely imprisoned behind our bars. In the
morning the nurses would enter wearing wellington
boots as they squelched through the snow at the
bottom of all beds. Happily most days and nights were
a bit warmer.

Depending on the time and day, the veranda had the

advantage, or disadvantage, of being out of earshot of the wireless that was high on the wall at one end of the ward. I have no idea of whether it was capable of being tuned to more than one station, as it was permanently set on the BBC Light Programme. All the popular music of the day was broadcast on this station and as the mid 1950s arrived so did pop charts. Long before the Beatles, another Liverpool born singer, Lita Roza, was producing hit records and her 1951 version of Allentown Jail remains one of the best available.

But in 1954 she released "How Much Is That Doggy In The Window?" The next line, oft repeated was "the one with the waggly tail" and it was in the charts for eleven weeks, which seemed like eleven years. For one week it was number one and the BBC played it again and again. I think at first I liked it, but then I grew irritated by the barking canine and eventually I became thoroughly bored with it. But there was no escape. All over the ward the dog barked and wagged its tail in the hope of a better life than being in the window. In later years I discovered that Lita Roza disliked the song as much as I did, and the only time she had ever sung it was at the recording.

The hospital staff had one overriding ambition, which was to help us to be as normal as possible. Their idea of normality was one I would challenge in later life, but I was far too young to question it then. Perhaps more significantly, I did not know that I was in any sense abnormal. I was disabled. My friends in hospital were disabled. Children were disabled: that was normal. Grown-ups were not disabled. This was perfectly obvious, because none of the adults we saw were disabled. The logic was simple. When you were a kid you had some parts of your body that didn't work, and as you grew up they might work or they might not.

When one side of the body is stronger than the other side there is a danger that the stronger muscles will distort the body, causing deformities. Efforts were taken to avoid this, but in my case they failed miserably and curvature of the spine was the result. Polio was shaping me, as well as my life.

The Holy Grail was to walk like other people. To this end a great deal of effort was expended. In my case both my legs were too weak to enable me to stand. The answer was to encase them in scaffolding, or so it seemed at the time. I was told it was time for me to wear callipers, but first I had to have the right shoes.

Unaware of the luxury I was to enjoy, I was told I would have my feet measured for my boots, and a man arrived to do just that. My foot was placed on a piece of paper and an outline taken with a cold pen. The boots would be made of leather with a wooden heel into which was drilled a hole. The bottom of the calliper would slot into the hole in the heel. The callipers themselves were made of steel and leather.

On each side was a steel bar that stretched from the heel to the groin. At the top they were linked by a round piece of metal covered in leather, and through this the leg was placed until the foot could be placed in the boot. Leather straps and a kneecap prevented the leg bending while the calliper was being worn. I remember the weight of those callipers. I have no idea which company made them, but I suspect it was the same company that built the Forth Bridge!

Equipped with a calliper on each leg and a pair of walking sticks, I was ready to learn to walk. This was difficult. Both legs were stiff, the sticks slipped on the polished floor and if the ferrule landed on a bit of dust there was no friction at all and a fall was inevitable. Fortunately, being small I did not have far to fall. But it was awkward. I could get about far more easily on the floor sliding on my bottom than I could carrying what seemed like a ton of iron around with me. But slowly I became accustomed to my steel legs and learnt to walk a few steps with the aid of walking sticks, later replaced by elbow crutches. I was to use this equipment throughout my childhood. The elbow crutches were improved, or so I was told, by being made so they could extend as I grew and would not need to be replaced. The problem with the improvement was that it consisted of one piece of tubing being inserted into the other and held in place with a clip that fitted through holes in the tubes. With use the holes stretched, so whenever the crutch hit the ground there was a metallic click as the clip hit the top of the hole. Click click, here comes the crip!

However, with the use of the callipers I was perpendicular. I was almost normal! But not normal enough. There is no end to the efforts to which our doctors will go to make us 'normal'. There was a problem with my left foot and muscles needed moving. At the age of four I was to have my first operation. Also at that tender age I had my first shave. No body hair must be near the site of the operation. Then I was covered with some magic potions to ensure I was sterile. Of course, I recall nothing of the operation apart from a huge black rubber mask being placed over my face and being told to count to 10. The smell of rubber was horrid, and I resisted in vain the gases pouring into my body.

When I awoke I was in pain, but I was told that was normal and I should not complain. I would soon be OK. I had other operations later in childhood and they were all as useful as this first one, which was no use at all.

Parents are in a dreadfully difficult position. They want to do what is best for their child, so they accept the advice of doctors who are supposed to know best. It is hardly surprising that my mum did what most mums do. She signed the consent for the operation.

Time passed as hospital routine followed hospital routine. I was approaching the age of five and was

soon to face the world on the other side of the bars
– that place where the fresh air lived! On my fifth
birthday the hospital had a party for me, and they must
have tipped off the press, because a picture of me
appeared in the local newspaper. Soon afterwards my
mum arrived to take me to a place called 'home'. It was
bye-bye to the hospital ward that had been my world,
and also bye-bye to the dog with the tail of perpetual
motion.

I was to grow to love the house and the area to
which my mother brought me, but my first impression
was one of shock that such places existed at all. My
family had moved to Tweed Street in the Newsham
Park area of Liverpool. At first the rooms seemed tiny.
I was used to the open spaces of the hospital and did
not know rooms as small as this existed. But there was
a real fire blazing in the fireplace, and Mum put me in
front of it. It was cosy and my family were all around
me. The small room was filled with happiness and
love. I was home, where I belonged.

Chapter 2

Greenbank

Before I was discharged from hospital, my parents had
moved to their own new rented council home. For most
of my childhood it was also mine. In truth, the house
was hardly new and was already almost 100 years old
when Mum, Dad and my sister Joan moved in.

The house and the tightly-packed terrace street
in which it was located were typical of streets
throughout Liverpool. When built there were no spaces
between the houses, but now there were gaps the
size of two or three houses which were known to all
as the "bombies", recalling the Second World War
German bombs when 681 aircraft sought to destroy

Liverpool in the May Blitz of 1941. These were the houses that would soon be described as slums, but for many families they were an improvement and enabled people to have their own home. They had three bedrooms and three rooms downstairs but no bathroom or, indeed, any bathing facilities. The toilet was a small, cold building at the end of the yard at the back of the house. Inside there was one sink and a single tap in the kitchen, which was universally known as the 'back kitchen'. The pipes delivering water were so narrow that if one neighbour put on their tap the next house had no water until the neighbour had finished.

A long tin tub hung on the wall of the back yard, and when we had a bath it was dragged into the back kitchen, where the water was heated in buckets on the stove. We bathed in front of the cooker, which had its door open to provide heat. After the water had been used by a number of people, the tub would be pulled into the back yard and used to swill the concrete ground. Personal hygiene was mostly conducted in the back kitchen, although I later discovered that in Liverpool's public baths it was possible to pay to use a bathtub.

The room we used most was the living room, known as the kitchen. Giving it this name was not entirely eccentric, as it housed the fireplace. This was a range and included an oven and a large black mantle. The oven gained its heat from the open fire. Every week the range had to be cleaned and "blackleaded". My first memory of Tweed Street is of this small room. Sitting on the floor in front of the open fire that blazed away happily spreading heat and colours across the room, I loved the direct heat. It was the first fire I had seen.

A dining table sat under the window that looked out onto the back yard. There was a settee and an easy chair that the rest of us could use only when Dad was out. This was his chair, and no one else had a right to use it. From the ceiling hung a wooden clothes maiden, from which damp clothes would be hung to dry, above the sideboard that completed the furnishing. There was no television, or even a socket into which to plug one.

Before the clothes were hung up, Mum would squeeze them through the mangle in the yard. This was no easy task as everything was done manually. When Mum did the ironing, the bulb was removed from the light socket and the iron would then be connected to it. It was light or ironing, never both simultaneously. Even this choice assumed there were coins available to feed into the electric meter. We were often plunged into darkness when "the shilling ran out".

The house was, in truth, a humble slum in an unassuming street in a working-class part of the city, but its small rooms found space for love, warmth and much happiness. Outside its door was another world waiting to be explored and mapped, and wider territories added for more exploration. But that would be for another day, because no sooner was I settling into my new home than I had to go to school. Not the school a few minutes' walk away that my brothers and sisters would later attend but one about five miles away in the south of the city.

I was not allowed the luxury of living at home for long. As World War II had ended, the Admiralty had decommissioned a school they had used to accommodate the Wrens who worked at the Western Approaches in central Liverpool and from which defence against U-boats in the Atlantic Ocean had been organised. Liverpool City Council agreed to lease it for 30 years and to use it as a residential school for disabled children. It was given the somewhat misleading title of 'The Children's Rest School of Recovery', though it was known to one and all locally as Greenbank.

At the time Liverpool City Council was following national guidelines on the education of disabled children. The Education Act 1944 separated children into categories. Those later described as having learning disabilities were defined as educationally sub-normal or maladjusted. I fell into the category of "physically handicapped", which sometimes overlapped with another category, "delicate". Although it was accepted that ideally disabled children should be educated alongside their peers in ordinary schools, a major consideration was whether the disabled child would interrupt the education given to other children. A brochure produced by the Liverpool Education Committee in 1957 states: "the aim of the special schools for physically handicapped children, whether day or boarding, is to alleviate and to cure their physical condition, and at the same time to bring the educational attainment to the highest standards compatible with their physical condition and mental ability."[2]

In singing the praises of special schools the same brochure says "in these schools he can be given a suitable education by teachers who specialise in this kind of work, he can be given expert medical and nursing attention, and, being among other handicapped children, he feels no sense of inferiority. He is happier and he is given the special training necessary to enable him to make a contribution to the community." I wish I had known at the time that I was supposed to be happy in this school.

Throughout life my abiding memory of this school is that I loathed the place and took as much time away from it as possible. Looking back, I am not sure why I

2. The Education of Handicapped Pupils, a brochure prepared by the Liverpool Teachers' Advisory Committee, March 1957.

hated it so much, because, although it was the most violent institution in which I ever stayed, there was also kindness and compassion. In many ways it was of its day and behaviour that would now attract the attention of the courts was viewed as matter of fact and normal.

The school was located on Greenbank Lane in an area of Liverpool that was and remains almost rural, although just a few miles from the city centre. It was between two parks, Sefton, the City's largest park, and Greenbank Park. Both had once been part of King John's deer park of Toxteth. My first impression was that it looked like a huge house but was much smaller than the hospital in which I had spent most of my life. It was of brown and red brick and had a surfeit of chimneys sprouting from its long roofs. It could accommodate 50 pupils, boys or girls, aged between 5-16.

Mum and Dad took me up the few steps leading to the front door. Yes, there were steps, in a school intended for disabled kids. There was an accessible entrance at the side of the building that led into the pantry. Beyond the large wooden front door was a small reception area on one side of which was a staircase. I was later to learn that this was where the staff went and where the headmistress lived. It was a no-go area. On the wall was a portrait of Eleanor Rathbone, the social reformer whose family owned the property and had always supported it. Facing the door was a corridor, and on the right side was the office of the headmistress who I now met for the first time. She was a stern, short and stout woman named, somewhat inappropriately, Miss Long. We never hit it off. The detailed memory of that first meeting has long since evaporated, but I recall her office, to which I was on many occasions summoned to receive punishment for real or imaginary misdemeanours. The next office contained her loyal school secretary, Miss G, a large and powerful woman who would "have no nonsense".

Near the end of the corridor was the kitchen, and at the end was the main hall. To the right was the dining room. The hall seemed massive, but as the school had only 50 pupils it did not need to be large and I only managed to put its scale into proportion later. It was not too big but large enough for its purposes.

An old lift, large enough for two wheelchair users, was located on the left when entering from the corridor. Naturally we kids were not allowed to use it unless we were with a member of staff. It was an easy rule to enforce because the metal gates were too heavy for most of us to open or close. The lift was slow and gentle, and outside it had a plaque commemorating the orthopaedic surgeon Sir Robert Jones, who had advised that when it moved the lift must not cause distress to people who had had surgery. Around the hall were the classrooms, and off to the left the medical facilities. Greenbank had two objectives. One was to provide basic education and the other was to ensure we remained healthy.

The lift led to a balcony that overlooked the hall and also provided a better view of the glass roof that ensured it enjoyed natural light. There were separate dormitories for boys and girls and each had about six beds. In those dorms I made friendships with other boys which would become lifelong. Although some of the pupils had significant impairments as a result of cerebral palsy, polio or similar conditions, others had slight asthma and were about as delicate as a docker's boot. I was soon to discover that bullying was rife. It was mostly led by boys who had been classified as delicate but who were as tough as they came and used to getting their own way.

I was well accustomed to seeing my parents for only a short time every week when they had visited me in hospital. Now I was to see even less of them. As I said my tearful farewells, I was informed that they would be back soon. In fact, visiting for parents was restricted to two hours once every two weeks. Each Wednesday we were required to write to our parents and assure them all was well. As teachers read the letters before being posted, they were not the place for saying how miserable I felt.

I soon settled into the ritualised routine of the school. The day started at seven in the morning. The birds in the woods alongside the school usually created an accurate alarm clock, and spring was marked by the arrival of the cuckoo with its distinctive call. Then ablutions, with care staff standing by to ensure necks were rubbed and the whole procedure done with cold water.

At eight came breakfast. We had to queue to enter, and before we passed from hall to dining room Miss Long stood on guard to check our hands were clean. I don't think I ever appreciated the food. Sometimes it was undercooked or overcooked, but we were required to eat what was placed in front of us and failure to do so might result in a visit to Miss Long's office. The common response was to hold our noses until we opened our mouths to gasp for air, and then the food would be forcefully spooned in. There could be no escape, as she wandered around the room checking on everyone and then did the same again. A goldfish in a glass bowl could not have been monitored so closely. At nine came assembly and prayers and then lessons.

It might be thought that with so few pupils we would have received individual attention, but in each class there were people of different ages and widely different intellects. Some pupils had had brain damage at birth and others were as bright or dim as they would have been if they had not been disabled. Despite this, the teachers were a determined lot and ensured we benefited from a general education. I was unable to assess how this compared to that given in what we knew as ordinary schools, but at the time it did not matter. Greenbank was our world.

This being long before Margaret Thatcher became Secretary of State for Education, at 10.30 we had a 15-minute break period, which started with drinking a third of a pint of milk. Thatcher abolished this in the early 1970s, which earned her the sobriquet 'Thatcher the Milk Snatcher'. Fancy, our little bottle of milk was to become political!

These breaks were spent in the hall, or if the weather permitted in the yard that ran alongside the school. Beyond the schoolyard was the caretaker's garden in which he grew vegetables that we would eventually eat. The caretaker was a remarkable man who seemed to be able to do anything, including making wooden wheelchairs. He built one for a boy who needed a great deal of support if he was to remain upright. The school also had a number of manufactured wood and wicker wheelchairs, and I enjoyed using these sometimes because I could go much faster than when I walked. They had two large wheels at the front and a small wheel at the back in a central position, which meant the chairs were unstable and could be easily turned over, but that was great fun.

Routine was all. Classes stopped at midday and lunch (we called it dinner) was served as soon as we had been to the toilet and washed our hands. Then we had to line up for the ritual inspection of hands.

Depending how long lunch took there was time to play, but only until one o'clock. Several rows of low canvas beds appeared in the hall, one for every pupil. This was the 'Rest' bit in the school's name. We had to rest on these beds for an hour a day. At first we were not even permitted to read a comic. For one hour we were required to rest. It was the most boring part of the day. What on earth were we meant to do? We were full of energy and lying doing nothing seemed a complete waste of time.

After what seemed three hours later this rest hour finally ended and at two o'clock it was back to classes. The school day finished at 4 pm and then an hour's play before dinner (which we called tea) at five. At 6 pm preparations started for going to bed. The dorms were lively because most of us were not tired. But soon the lights went off.

Eventually we were allowed to read during the rest period. I recall reading Enid Blyton's "Famous Five" books. It did not seem to me remarkable that so many of them went to boarding schools but there was no mention of them having to have a rest period.

In addition to the daily routine, the weeks had their own pattern to follow. Clean clothes were placed at the foot of our beds every Wednesday and Sunday. Apart from underwear, always white, everything seemed to be grey, although there was no official school uniform.

Saturdays would start with the Light Programme's

'Children's Favourites', introduced by Uncle Mac. Later in the morning we would be taken to a newsagent/ sweet shop called Luxtons in Smithdown Road. We were given 6d each (worth about 60 pence in 2015 values) and with such riches we could buy three or four items. Luxtons has changed hands several times, but it is still there with another name over it. Mr Luxton also sold rubber bands, essential raw material for making a catapult.

Saturdays were the time to escape the schoolyard and use the paddock beyond it. This large field had trees and bushes at its side. The first was a source of wood for catapults and the bushes provided a place to be out of the view of adults, or so we thought. At one time the paddock also contained a couple of horses owned by a teacher. It was considered a privilege to be able get up early and to help brush the parts of the horses that could be reached.

As many of the vegetables were grown by the caretaker, Saturday was also the time we were enrolled into kitchen duties, which often meant podding peas.

Sunday inevitably meant a visit to church. The church in question was St Barnabas's at the end of Penny Lane and opposite the bus shelter later made famous by the Beatles. This was no Sunday school but a full service aimed at adults, and at the age of five I learnt that I was not allowed to kill people or commit adultery, whatever that was. We would each be given a penny to place in the plate when it came around, along with instructions not to remove any of the cash already accumulated. In summer we would be made to walk to the church, but if the weather was poor the school mini-bus would make several trips.

The school had a close relationship with St Barnabas's and every Christmas they organised a party for us, which included Santa and presents. Indeed so many different groups wanted to give us parties that Christmas was crowded with them. Each brought their Father Christmas, who had changed shape from the week previous. One always smelt of something strange and one of the older boys explained it was brown ale from an alehouse. Most mysterious!

The weekends were also the time we were permitted to watch television, which was not in the hall but in a small room off it. The size of the room made it impossible for everyone to fit into it, but for most programmes there was sufficient space for those who wished to watch. Westerns were common and after 'Boots and Saddles' or similar programmes ended it was common to see a few boys gallop across the hall slapping one buttock to make their trusty steed race faster while the other hand held the imaginary reins to their fanciful horse. This was not for me alas, because I had both legs encased in full-length callipers as neither leg could bear my weight. Speed and these heavy metal and leather callipers were incompatible. Even when using my crutches falls were frequent, but they usually caused no damage, although bad falls also happened, and they were painful. The callipers were functional and well made, but they could not bend at the knee. This meant my legs were held in a straight position all day and this caused some pain that was only relieved at night when I could take them off and bend my legs. They also made it more difficult to use chairs, because having two straight legs made it easier to sit on the edge of a chair than to sit back with my iron legs before me. So my steed stayed firmly in the stable.

It took me some time to realise that we had the benefit of television long before most families in Liverpool could contemplate renting one, let alone buying one. We also received more toys at Christmas than many families could afford for the entire family.

Saturday night also became film night. We were not taken to the cinema, but instead a projector was placed in the dining room and a screen erected. It was at one of these sessions that I first saw "Reach for the Sky" detailing the life of Douglas Bader, played by Kenneth More. Bader had famously returned to being a fighter pilot after losing both legs. The projector was a gift from the crew of the ship the *Empress of England*, which had regular sailings between Liverpool and Montreal. One day we were invited to visit the ship, and thus I had my first sight of what luxury looked like. I recall the crew made us very welcome and laid on a slap-up feast.

Like the seasons, Greenbank had its own rhythm. During the summer months there would be a number of school outings. Many of these were educational and were to local places such as North Wales. The best one each year had nothing to do with education – it was just fun. The Littlewoods Organisation sponsored an annual day trip to Southport, about 20 miles north of Liverpool. All the special schools in Liverpool could benefit from this. As well as having a large beach, Southport also boasted the best fairground in the area and each child would be given 20 tickets so they could have 20 rides free of charge. This seemed generous, but we could easily use those tickets before the day was half done. This was not a major problem, because teachers always seemed to have a supply of additional tickets and the fairground staff were soon demonstrating the spirit of the day. Frequently they gave us back our tickets, so we could use them on another ride. The problem was not getting free rides on the fair but remembering where we had to get to and by what time to receive our picnic lunch. This was a day we looked forward to all year and to be denied it would be a major blow.

One year this threat hung over us. A new teacher had joined the school. I do not recall much of her apart from the fact that she was Welsh and introduced us to Tolkien's *The Hobbit.* One day she was on the evening duties and so would patrol the dormitories. As a joke a few of the fitter boys put a box on the top of the door, which was ajar. In it were placed surgical boots and other items. We waited in anticipation and as the door slowly opened, the box fell onto the head and shoulders not of the teacher but of the head teacher, Miss Long.

A look of anger contorted her face. She stood for a few moments rapidly fluttering her eyelids and said, "Who is responsible for this outrage?" Naturally, nobody owned up. Next day all those in the dormitory were required to sit in the hall until we revealed the culprits. We were informed that if we failed to do so none of us would be permitted to go on the Southport outing. This was a dire threat, but we all knew that anybody who dared to speak would endure months of bullying by the school thugs. Even missing Southport was better than that, but in the end the threat came to nothing and off to Southport we all went.

The unusual aspect of this incident is that none of us received physical punishment. Normally, the slightest breaking of the school rules would result in an assault, either immediate or delayed. When the punishment came immediately, it was usually in the form of heavy slapping to any part of the body that could be reached. The obvious place would be the legs, but as so many of us wore metal callipers, attempting to hit our legs was likely to hurt the hand of the member of staff. Bottoms, backs, arms and the face became targets. On one occasion I was in the dining room sitting on a chair at the table when I received a violent smack across my face from behind. It was so strong I was lifted off the chair, slid on the floor and ended up near the radiator. Having had the punishment, the charge came in a flurry of saliva from Miss Long. "That's for swearing at Miss W yesterday." To this day I cannot recall whether I was guilty of this misdemeanour, but it is possible, as I was frequently arguing with teachers and attendants. It is equally possible it was somebody else, as being blamed and punished for somebody else's actions was by no means unusual. It seemed that somebody had to be punished and it didn't much matter who it was. Some pupils were automatically exempt, but I wasn't one of them.

Nor was Arthur, one of my close friends. He looked Afro-Caribbean, although I later discovered that his birth mother was white British. He had been fostered by a remarkable woman, Mrs Pendleton, and had thus joined a large and loving family. I was later to know much of this family, who always treated Arthur and his friends with warmth and kindness. Like me, Arthur had had polio. His legs were weak, although he could walk with the aid of callipers. His left arm comprised little more than skin and bone. There was no muscle. His right arm was unaffected and strong. It needed to be.

Arthur was funny, outspoken and a brilliant mimic of our head teacher. He was also independent minded and seemed to offend the staff even more than I did. There were many occasions when they sought to punish him in public, but if they tried to hit him he would use his strong arm to fight back and punch them. This invariably resulted in reinforcements arriving and there were many times when Arthur was on the floor of the dining room with one or two members of staff kneeling on him and seeking to slap him. They seldom succeeded in pinning down his wild right arm, which would lash out in all directions to knock them off. Although he received many blows, he delivered a goodly number in response.

When punishment was pre-planned it normally meant a trip to Miss Long's office to receive the charge and several lashes of the cane across the hand to encourage better behaviour in future. I recall one time when I was subjected to this correction that Miss Long took careful aim to ensure the blow fell across my palm, but when the cane swished down she caught me across the wrist. Although this was painful it was better than having my palm damaged, because I was using elbow crutches and would have no choice but to have put weight onto the wheals on the palm. It takes a degree of insensitivity to cane a person's hand when that same hand has to be used to bear weight when using crutches.

There was not much I could do about staff violence, but there was still the issue of bullying to cope with. Soon after I arrived at the age of five I could see this was a danger and a problem. I was one of the weaker kids and an obvious victim. I soon made friends with other boys who were more than capable of defending themselves and, by extension, me. Joe had cerebral palsy that affected his legs, but he had the arms of an athlete. When one of the school bullies decided to give me a hard time Joe intervened and gave him a bloody nose with one punch of his fist. That reduced trouble from that quarter, but it was always wise to avoid the bullies. One day we heard the main offenders were to be moved to a school for maladjusted children. Not many tears were shed.

Although my strongest recollections of the school related to the perpetual violence, or a nagging expectation of it, many of the staff were kind and caring. Attendants would often bring in books and comics for us. They were largely local women who had children of their own. It was their job to ensure we were ready for whatever we had to do, and they were ever present. As we dressed they were in the dorms and helped those who were unable to dress without help.

They were there in the washrooms and when we had baths. If we were out in the sun, they would ensure each of us wore a sun hat.

Some of them became almost surrogate mothers. One of the teachers, who seldom missed an opportunity to physically punish a child, showed another side when a pupil was ill. She became as tender and caring as a saint. She clearly believed that if she spared the rod she would spoil the child. When I spoke with her many years later it was clear that she bore no child malice but thought it was important that she prepared us for later life, and in some ways she did. We certainly learnt how to survive. Well, some us of did.

Visiting time on alternate Sundays was something to look forward to. Apart from seeing our parents we knew that we could not get slaps across the face for some days before, because the bruises might cause questions to be asked.

Getting to the school was difficult for my parents. They did not own a car and often could not afford the bus fare, but they would never leave me without a visit. Although Dad came sometimes, it was usually Mum with my sister Joan. It was over five miles to the school from home and often they walked there and back. Some of the other kids had parents with cars. Miss Long always made a beeline for such parents at visiting time to talk about their child. She hardly ever came near my mum and me. Mum commented on this many times. She would say, "I don't care. She's only interested in the posh ones", but she clearly felt slighted. Given the effort she made to get to the school she should have been shown more respect.

When four o'clock arrived and visitors were required to leave, most of us by then had pockets full of sweets. Once all visitors had left we were required to hand over our sweets, which were then given to us in small portions over the next fortnight. Even kids who had no sweets seemed to acquire a supply, and it became clear that the school did not recognise ownership and sweets were owned in common. One of my first lessons in socialism!

Medicine and doctors were very much part of school life. As in all schools of the time, the school nurse would visit regularly to check for life-threatening illnesses such as nits in the hair. Everybody lived in close proximity, so if one child caught measles it would quickly spread to all others and the "sick bay" became crowded. Every now and then the school would be placed in quarantine because of some bug doing the rounds, but generally speaking, although many pupils had severe impairments we were otherwise fairly healthy and robust. When quarantine applied, parents were not allowed to visit.

One of the recommended treatments for polio was hydrotherapy. Although the school had once boasted its own swimming pool, it had long since been filled in. Twice a week Miss Long would take Arthur and me in the school Morris Traveller to Fazakerley Hospital in north Liverpool, nine miles away. Once there we changed and then entered the water, which was almost as warm as having a hot bath. The head physiotherapist, Miss Allen, always started off with breathing lessons. "Breathe in deeply. Now out slowly, slowly." Then arms and legs were exercised. The joy of doing this in a warm pool was that moving weak limbs was so much easier than on dry land. Gravity disappeared, and limbs became lighter. After exercise we were allowed to mess around in the pool for another 10 or 15 minutes and then we took off our swimming trunks or costumes and clambered out of the pool naked. Although I have no doubt that these hydrotherapy sessions were enormously beneficial, it did mean missing the equivalent of almost a full day of school each week.

There were also other medical appointments. Every six months I would be seen by the consultant, Mr O'Malley, who always wore smart suits and highly-polished shoes. He was not one for talking to his young patients but mostly spoke to Miss Long. Most of what he said was literally and metaphorically over my head, but I soon learnt the phrases that indicated trouble ahead. If he said, "I would like to see his parents", it meant he wanted me to have an operation and he needed Mum to agree. I had several operations as a child but could never see the value of any of them. They just meant massive amounts of pain, long spells in hospital and being in institutions with even less freedom than the school.

Medical students usually surrounded Mr O'Malley. When he referred to me it was seldom by my name. "This is a left deltoid", he would say, leaving me mystified. I later discovered that the deltoid is the muscle that covers the top of the shoulder. It was also one of the muscles that polio had destroyed, so I did not have one. My identity was not only lost to a muscle but to a muscle I did not have. I soon grew accustomed to doctors behaving as though they were gods who could lord it over us mere mortals. My respect for them waned with each medical intervention that seemed to me to be a waste of time and produced no improvement. Looking back, I think I was content with how I was, but the doctors had some vision of normality that they wanted me to achieve.

I had one operation when I was 10 or 11 at the now-demolished Southern Hospital. I was in Horsefall Ward, which in many ways was a good location because it had views over the River Mersey, which at the time was new to me. I recall that when I was able to walk with my right leg in plaster of Paris I asked if I could see the operating theatre where I had had my operation, and two nurses took me to it. They showed me the surgical instruments, which even then were small. I foolishly said, "I thought they would be dirty big things." They feigned shock. "Dirty? Nothing in here is dirty!" They were right of course, because before any operation most of my body was shaved and wrapped in dressings. At least I was clean. Again more schooling was missed. But why did hospitals always smell the same and have walls painted in grubby green and cream colours, as they did in the 1950s?

The school employed a physiotherapist, Mr Kirby, who had been blinded in the war. I would have two sessions a week with him. To this was added games sessions and, of course, physical exercise. This was a gentle session, until a new PE teacher arrived. In the school paddock the Essex apparatus appeared. It consisted of climbing frames in different shapes and sizes designed to enable all the pupils to use it. I think some of us would have been a profound disappointment to the designers, because although we could get on to the bottom rung we made little progress after that. The school hall could also be used for PE lessons, and ropes would be hung from the rafters so people could climb them. One boy, Gerry, was unable to use his legs much, but he had powerful arms and could climb the rope easily and then walk on his hands along the rafter. Understandably, he later enjoyed success as a Paralympian wheelchair basketball player. Equally significantly, long after the school had closed and becoming derelict, Gerry started a project to turn it into a training centre for disabled people, and did so very successfully. I could not copy him. When I tried to climb the rope I was incapable of getting my feet off the ground.

Even as a young child I began to question whether all this medical intervention was necessary. It was never fun. I had a friend of my own age, Spike. He had cerebral palsy and his limbs were difficult to control, but somehow he managed. He was a huge fan of Alma Cogan, a pop star of the day. One day Spike told me he was going into hospital to have his arms sorted out. Spike never returned to the school, as he died in hospital. A few of us discussed the loss of Spike and decided he had not needed the operation but had it so that he would fit in with his parents' view of what he should look like. Someone said, "He died while they tried to make him match the furniture at home." This was a bit harsh, but in me it struck a chord. Why were we disabled kids always meant to adapt to a world that could not make us welcome? Later in life this question kept returning, and slowly I found an answer. We should not be expected to do all the adapting.

In the late 1950s Ron McManus arrived on the scene; he was to become a lifelong friend. He started a Scout troop at the school, known as the 17th Wavertree. I was too young to join the Scouts, but he also established a Cub pack, which I did join. Suddenly

I was involved in activities that I could do with a degree of competence and my success was invariably rewarded with a badge, until my sleeves were covered in them. Next to the school was a small woodland, which seemed like a forest to us. Here we could light campfires and cook sausages. Weekends away from school were organised to Tawd Vale, a camping ground owned by Liverpool Scouts, near Ormskirk. This was a much better way of spending a Sunday than waiting to put a penny on the plate in church.

When I left Greenbank at the age of 11 I still returned each Friday evening to attend Scouts. Scouting became a large part of my teenage years. Ron McManus understood boys perfectly and added adventure to our lives. One consequence was that we all became much more independent and able to cater for ourselves. Mac's wife, Dot, set up a Guide troop.

Another initiative the school introduced was the Wednesday Club. This was run by one of the teachers, Mr Forbes, who taught me to play chess. He was a proud Scot who also introduced us to Scottish folk music. It was worth joining the club, because members could stay up later.

When I was about 10 I was invited to join my first committee, although that was rather a grand title for a gaggle of lads meeting in a corner. It was known as the Escape Committee. We were not concerned with digging tunnels or getting people across enemy lines, but there was always somebody who wanted to "do the bunk", usually to go home. This predictability of destination was the weakness in our schemes, because the police always knew where to go to capture the escapee. Our job was to help the person get out of the school premises, ensure they had enough money for bus fares and know where the bus stops where and what bus they should get. Somehow the older boys seem to possess all this information. I was usually given the task of causing a distraction, as the easiest way out meant passing the school secretary's window. If a fight started in the corridor she was unable resist the temptation to run out, separate us and start administering punishment. While she was so engaged a pupil would be skipping or hobbling passed her window, heading for freedom!

I once took this action myself, but I only got as far as Sefton Park before a police car pulled alongside me and asked if I was Herbert. When I denied it, they smiled and told me to get in. They then took me for a short drive, bought me some sweets and returned me to the school to face the music.

In 1960 escaping from the school suddenly became easier. In June of that year a Liverpool department store, Henderson's, caught fire. It started early in the afternoon and spread rapidly. Although 20 engines attended, 11 people lost their lives. It is thought that it was started by an electrical fault. Greenbank responded instantly. The classrooms downstairs were turned into dormitories and the dormitories into classrooms. In each dormitory emergency evacuation doors were fitted, and they could be easily opened by any of the stronger pupils. Upstairs, chutes were installed so children could quickly slide to the bottom floor without needing to use the lift.

I missed a fair amount of time at Greenback because we were allowed home for school holidays. When the holidays ended I was never keen to return, and my parents never insisted. In some cases, my mum had good reasons because she was required to ensure I had the appropriate clothes, which she could not afford. After a week or so a man from what was known as the School Board, Mr Broster, arrived. His job was to get me back to school, but he was well accustomed to families being unable to afford to clothe their children. He would therefore provide vouchers so Mum could buy the clothes. Sometimes he would drive me to the school, thus saving Mum a complicated bus journey and its associated costs. As I grew older and spent more time at home I was able to experience life in the street in which I lived.

Tweed Street ran parallel to Berwick Street. It was a cul-de-sac, at the end of which my family lived. At the far end was West Derby Road, which linked the area of Fairfield with the city centre. Today it is a dual carriageway with limited character, but then it was shop lined and at the end of the street was a car sales garage that also sold fuel.

About a quarter of the way down, the street was crossed by Proctor Street, which linked with Berwick Street. At the other end there was a small woodyard from which the smell of wet and cut wood would seep.

Within a few minutes' walk, most of the necessities of life could be easily obtained. At the junction of Tweed Street and Proctor Street was Mary Brown's general shop, which seemed to sell everything apart from food. If medication was needed late at night when the shop had long closed, rapping at the door would bring Mary to her bedroom window and the tablets would be thrown down, on the mutual understanding that they would be paid for the following day.

As a young child I thought West Derby Road was sufficiently far away to be in another world. Proctor Street was a limit of my universe. If I turned left, the Berwick pub was on the corner of Berwick Street. Turning right on Berwick Street led to the forbidden world of the main road, but a left turn led to Malone's grocery shop where I would be sent to buy eggs or loaves. The ends of the two streets were linked by an entry or alleyway which was just wide enough for a small car to drive along. Once back in Tweedy, Boaler Street could be reached via another entry or alleyway, but this one was wide enough for pedestrians only. However, it was worth travelling along this entry because it led to Proctor's sweetshop on Boaler Street. These two entries were so much part of everyday life that each had its own name – they were the 'fat entry' and the 'thin entry'.

A small park that had been created by the council in 1862 when Shiel Road was constructed completed this little world. The 15 acres between this road and Tweed Street was named after Richard Shiel, the first Irish alderman to serve on the town council. Even earlier there had been a zoo sharing this site and the larger Newsham Park that was on the other side of Shiel Road. I got to know this small patch of Liverpool extremely well. At this time I was walking using two iron callipers and elbow crutches.

Most people when they walk look ahead. I had to do the same, but much of my attention was spent looking at the ground. The rubber tips or ferrules at the ends of walking sticks or crutches were badly designed in those days. If they failed to stop the crutch slipping, a fall was inevitable and the crutches would behave differently according to the surface. At school most of the floors comprised wooden blocks arranged symmetrically. Although the floors were kept clean they were not highly polished and provided reasonable friction and grip. Grass or rough concrete was even better. Along the pavements of Tweed Street the paving stones were rough concrete and provided excellent grip. The street was covered in tarmac that hid the cobbles beneath it, and that also provided excellent grip.

The problem was the entries or alleyways. The fat entry leading to Malone's was laid with large cobblestones. I'm sure that at one time horses found these extremely helpful when pulling their loads, but the cobbles were smooth and rounded. When they were wet my crutches would glide across the top and it took great skill to guide the ferrules to the deepest part between the cobblestone over which I was slipping and the next one. If I got this right I could regain my balance before my crutch flew away from me, leaving me with nothing to do but to try and break the fall. It did have the advantage of being flat and not on a hill or slope.

The entry to Proctor's was up an incline with a gully running along the side. The paving flags were smooth, like York stone, and had limited adhesive qualities. Coming down this entry was much more dangerous than going up it, because gravity was already trying to make my crutches misbehave. A stray piece of paper, dust or water was all it took to ensure I once again bounced off the ground. In later years this was the entry I had to use to get to Boaler Street, where a school bus would pick me up to take me to school. When there was snow or ice on the ground Mum would go ahead of me, putting her foot in front of my crutch so it did not slip.

Defeating surfaces has been one of my tasks for life. Grass or soil is good when walking but difficult when using a wheelchair. Paving stones are hardly ever fitted at the same height, so sticks and crutches can easily catch and result in a fall. As a young child, falling was not too painful unless I banged my head, but as I grew older and heavier they caused more problems. When I later used wheelchairs, I soon noticed that every slight change in the surface was reflected in the ride, and a smooth ride out of doors was rare indeed.

The house became more crowded as the family increased in size with the arrivals of two sisters, Georgina and Jean. Eventually, there would be eight children. Somehow, there was always room. But we always knew that money was tight, although I do not recall feeling poor. Meals were simple, stews were common and a snack might be a jam or even a sugar butty. A butty was the local word for a sandwich. If we were short of bread there was always a neighbour ready to provide something.

Years later I was informed by people who claimed to know about such things that in the 1950s disabled people were segregated and lived in institutions. These were certainly the days of large hospitals for people with mental health issues, but there was not much segregation in our street. On one side of our house lived two sisters and their brother. One of the sisters had one leg much shorter than the other and wore a built-up shoe. The brother had epilepsy. On the other side lived a profoundly deaf woman and her brother, who wore a mask where his nose had once been. Across the street lived another man with epilepsy. These were just the people I knew who were disabled. Others might have had invisible disabilities. I never regarded having a disability as being exceptional. But unlike what I had believed in the hospital, I had learned that adults could also be disabled.

Most activities took place in the house or in the street. There were so few cars it was safe to use the entire street as a playground. Moreover, in Liverpool's tight-knit streets we were always under the watchful eye of a number of adults who stood on their front steps chatting or scrubbing the step. All the steps were immaculate and were scrubbed frequently. The games were simple games of childhood that usually required no more equipment than a ball of one size or another. Football was common but could lead to neighbours insisting we played somewhere else, as they feared the ball might go through one of their windows. For understandable reasons I was not terribly good at football, but I was usually given the role of goalkeeper on the understanding that I might hit the ball with one of my crutches. I was usually more successful as a goalpost, because if I could move fast enough a certain goal might hit the post instead!

Ve were living in slums, but each family was houseproud. I recall Mum polishing the lino in our lobby one day. As I tried to enter, the ferrule on my elbow crutch found no friction and slid away with me following it, banging my head against the door as I fell. The lino was polished no more.

The school holidays were an opportunity to get to know my parents and the increasing number of sisters. Mum was prepared to do almost anything for me, but Dad had other ideas. He was anxious that I should become as independent as possible. If he thought I could do something for myself, he insisted that I did so. There was to be no mollycoddling. He seemed to have the idea that if only I applied myself I could learn to walk without using the crutches. He fell into the same trap as many non-disabled people do, which is to judge a disabled person's success by the degree to which they do not appear to be disabled. He was not ashamed of my disability or me, and would often take me to Liverpool Museum or other attractions. But he still had an aspiration for me to be what he viewed as normal. In pursuit of this quest he erected two ropes down the back yard, so they resembled the parallel bars in a physiotherapy department. He would put me at the far end of the yard and not allow me to enter the house until I had walked the full length of the yard. Even if it was raining he would not relent. Although I disagree with my Dad's ambition, there is no doubt that his approach taught me to survive and become reasonably independent.

Dad had been a child during World War II but was not evacuated. When he left school at the age of 14 he became a carter, in the days when wagons were pulled around Liverpool's docks by horses. Although not a docker, much of his work in subsequent years seemed to be related to the docks. He had long periods of unemployment, but when he was working he did not give Mum much of his wages. Even when times were hard, he always had a good suit for when he went out and could always afford to frequent our local pub, the Berwick. Outside the house he was always friendly and cheerful to everyone he met and invariably helpful. Behind his closed door he was very conscious of his role as head of the household and expected to be waited on and obeyed. In this he was typical of many working-class men of the time. Inside their homes they could demand the respect the outside world seldom conferred on them.

Dad missed out on being a wealthy man. My paternal grandfather had been something of a wheeler-dealer in the scrap metal business, but what profits he made following the war seemed to be spent on beer. In contrast his brother Charlie became a successful scrap dealer and as I grew up C R Massie was a well-known name in the city. Granddad would sometimes turn up pushing a cart loaded with old clothes he had collected in exchange for balloons and the like. Having a rag and bone man in the family had an element of fun to it.

Mum had been evacuated to Ludlow during the war and although she had happy memories of the large house in which she stayed, and for the rest of her life told stories about the ghosts that also occupied the ancient place, she returned to Liverpool before the war ended. She and Dad married when they were 18. Her father was a seaman and spent the war as a chef on ships crossing to and from the United States. He always had the ability to open an empty cupboard and produce a meal from the contents. Long before Harry Potter, magic was thriving.

Grandma was a larger than life figure. After Granddad died she would end up at our house after a few drinks and stay the night. This usually meant in or on the bed I used, as my brothers had not yet arrived to share it.

There was a joyous chaos about the family home, with a steady stream of visitors. Towards the end of the week the debt collectors would arrive as many goods were bought on credit (this was long before credit cards). The local dairy was on Boaler Street and the owner, Mr Swift, also arrived for payment. Another visitor was Mr Constantine from Freeman's department store, which sold furniture. There was a steady stream of such people, including one who wanted Mum to pay for my surgical boots. Priority was always given to the rent man. The rent always had to be paid. None of these men were threatening and some were viewed almost as respected family friends, even though they sometimes had to wait to get paid. It was so much more interesting than life at school, but this disjointed life between boarding school and home was to end.

I have never been convinced about the supernatural and have never, as far as I am aware, seen a ghost. But there is one incident I cannot explain. Most of my dreams when sleeping at Greenbank were nightmares, and I can still recall some of them. One night I had a very different dream. I was leaving Greenbank and the place I was going to had a metal sculpture on the wall of two hands almost joined at the wrist with the fingers opening like the petals of a flower waiting to welcome a bee. I wrote to Mum telling her I thought I would be leaving Greenbank. I had been asking her for years to get me out of the place.

About two weeks later Miss Long approached me in class and said, "That silly dream you had. You will be leaving Greenbank at the end of term." Had she read the letter and decided to force the issue with the Education Department to be rid of me? I had never before been to the school to which I was sent next but when I first arrived the sight that caught my eyes was the sculpture of the silver hands on the wall of the school.

Chapter 3

Expanding Horizons

My departure from Greenbank was influenced by many
factors, but I suspect the main one was that Liverpool
City Council opened a new school for disabled children
in 1961. It formally opened in May of that year and I
became a pupil in September. It was named Sandfield
Park, after the original park in which it is located. I do
not recall how many pupils it catered for but think it
was about 75. More importantly, it was not a boarding
school but a day school, so disabled children travelled
to it from across the city.

Each day the 622 school bus would stop for me
outside Proctors' sweet shop on Boaler Street. Initially

the buses were the old Routemaster type, which were entered from the rear. They had a high step that I could not climb but there was always a member of staff on the bus to help or, more accurately, to simply lift me on. By the time the bus arrived for me it was already quite full, with a group of girls attending another special school. Somebody told me they were maladjusted, but my memory of them is that they were lively, boisterous and wonderful travelling companions. The journey to and from school was an important part of the day. If I seemed to be missing out on any aspect of life, one or other of the girls would be sure to enlighten me.

One day I was asked, "Have you heard this great new group that's playing at the Cavern?" When I replied, "No, I haven't", I was instantly instructed "Ar 'ey, Bert, you've got to go and see the Beatles at the Cavern. They're dead good." Despite this excellent advice, by the time I eventually entered the Cavern, navigating myself on crutches down the narrow flight of steps and leaning against a wall that was damp with condensation, the Beatles had long gone on to some place called fame and stardom.

Buses arrived at Sandfield at much the same time, like friends eager to greet each other, and this led to organised chaos as they jostled for a parking space. Once the Sandfield kids had been helped off, the buses left to deliver their remaining passengers to the appropriate schools.

Sandfield was nothing like my previous school. As far as I can recall there was no violence or any necessity for it. The teachers had an air of authority that commanded respect but also affection. My class teacher was Mr Melia. I was sitting near the back of the class, and one day he asked me to read a word on the blackboard. Whatever it was, I got it hopelessly wrong. He never said anything, but at the end of the class he asked me to stay behind and to sit at the front. He then wrote a word on the blackboard and asked me to read it, which I did successfully. He smiled and said, "I thought so. Your reading is not the problem. I think you need glasses. I'll arrange for the school nurse to see you." As a result I was soon wearing spectacles all day. But this gentle approach was so typical of him. He also had a tin of sweets he called his "magic tin", because regardless of how many he gave out as rewards the tin was never empty.

As I write, China is becoming a world power, both economically and militarily. I am reminded of the woodwork and crafts teacher, Mr Fellowes. All his lessons were absorbing as we learnt to make bookcases and other products from wood. We also messed around with clay, but my efforts to produce something with a symmetrical shape would have filled anyone with shame. He often warned us, "Remember that the Bible says one day yellow people will rule the earth." Does the Bible really say this?

Getting around the school was easy because the classrooms were in one of three corridors, the head teacher's office and the administration department were on another corridor and the rest of the school was taken up with the main hall and toileting facilities.

The head teacher, Mrs Fairhurst, was involved in all aspects of school life and I found her very supportive. She encouraged us to get involved in current affairs, but in 1962 it was difficult not to be interested in such matters as in the autumn of that year every newspaper and television news programme was filled with what became known as the Cuban Missile Crisis. At just 13 I was convinced we were heading for a nuclear war, and although I was not entirely sure what that entailed, it was bound to be bad. Decades later it became clear that had the United States not been blessed by having a President as wise as John Kennedy the crisis might not have been averted, but it stimulated my interest in current affairs and politics.

There seemed to be a constant stream of visitors to the school. I recall the Lord Mayor arriving and looking most important in a morning suit and emerging from a large civic car. We also had a visit from the comedian and actor Norman Wisdom. We all knew about his battles with "Mr Grimsdale", so he was a very welcome guest.

The education at Sandfield was similar to the education offered in secondary schools of the time, but, as at Greenbank, I missed much of it because of medical appointments. My hydrotherapy treatment continued, but instead of Miss Long being the chauffeur, the local ambulance service inherited the task. As I lived close to the ambulance depot, I was usually the first to be picked up. The ambulance had seats but no stretcher and was essentially providing a taxi service. In those days ambulances were not fitted with lifts, so I had to be lifted in manually. We would then tour the city picking up other disabled boys, all of whom had the same impairment as me, on the way to Fazakerley Hospital.

One of them was John, who lived near Scotland Road, then a Catholic part of the city. John and his parents were convinced that one day he would be cured. To this end every couple of years he went to Lourdes in France seeking a miracle. It never happened. I never understood this quest for a cure, as it seemed to be a complete waste of time. The cards had been dealt and we needed to play them the best we could. This became a debate in later years. Should disabled people seek cures or seek to ensure the world catered for our needs? Another boy lived near Goodison Park, home of Everton Football Club. He was Ken Robinson, who later in life became a celebrated educationalist and author and was awarded a knighthood. Of the five disabled working-class boys on those ambulance journeys, two were eventually knighted. If anybody had placed a bet on that happening, his or her winnings would have been a small fortune!

Despite enjoying the school and the friends I made there, life was still to some extent disjointed. My friends at school lived all over the city and we could only see each other at school. My sisters and brothers went to their school with other kids in the area and had them to play with after-school. My small circles of friends depended entirely on my current location. I was fortunate in being part of a large family that continued to grow. After Georgina there was Jean, and then Lenny, Wayne, Lynn and eventually Rodney. With Dad out and Mum working in the evenings in a sweet factory, until she went to work as a school cleaner, during the day it was my elder sister Joan who seemed to run the household in their absence, and she did so with great skill.

My circumstances were changing. After an operation on my right foot at the Southern Hospital I was discharged with a plaster of Paris covering part of my foot and the bottom of my right leg. This meant I could not use the calliper that normally covered the leg. I found I could manage without it because when using the elbow crutches I could take weight on my left leg, which was still in a full-length calliper, and then on my arms rather than my right leg.

Thus equipped, one day I set off to meet my first

celebrity and television star, Bob Monkhouse. He presented the television show "Candid Camera", which I thought was the funniest show on TV. By this time my family rented a TV, but like the gas and electricity it was operated via a meter on the back. If the cash ran out, the television would not operate until it received a meal of coins. I heard Monkhouse was opening a record shop on Kensington, which was about half a mile away. By this time I had outgrown the geographic limits of infancy and extended my boundaries. A half-mile walk was challenging, but if I allowed sufficient time it should be possible.

Off I went and managed to fall only twice on the way and although I could get up on my own, it was a bit of an ordeal. Happily, on both occasions an adult was near and quickly put me back on my feet, or, more precisely, on my foot. When I reached the shop there was a crowd of people waiting to get in, but somehow Monkhouse saw me and gestured to me that I should go to the front. When I did he said, "You look cold. Go into that room and somebody will give you a hot drink. I'll come in in a few minutes." One of the staff gave me a small cup of tea and eventually, after much longer than a few minutes, the great man appeared. He spent five or 10 minutes talking to me and signed his autograph on a photograph that he also gave me. It was only many years later that I learnt Monkhouse's eldest son, Gary, was disabled. In the 1990s, when I was heading a disability charity in London, Monkhouse assisted us in raising funds.

The winter of 1963 was hard. It was horribly and bitterly cold; Baltic in every sense. The first snow fell in Tweed Street in November and refused to melt until the end of March. Snow fell on ice and then froze, and the new ice was in turn covered with new snow. Even when the snow stopped falling, the ice maintained its grip on the ground. It was going nowhere.

In the bone-chilling cold, the limitations of our house became strikingly obvious. The fire in the kitchen struggled to heat the room. It needed to keep producing flames, but it was costly to keep loading it with coal, a supply of which was kept under the stairs. When the fire failed it had to be revitalised. The Liverpool Echo, such a useful paper, would have its pages scrunched up to get the fire started. Then a shovel would be placed in front of the fire and more pages of the Echo placed across it to help draw in air to the bottom of the fire. No other room in the house had any heat at all apart from the back kitchen where the cooker lived; when being used it would give a little heat.

Visiting the toilet down the yard was a nightmare and the ordeal of sitting on the frozen wooden seat ensured no one lingered. All the bedrooms were icy and frozen moisture hugged the inside as well as the outside of the windows. Although we slept three to a bed there was not much warmth to be had. On top of the blankets we placed old coats for extra warmth, but they were so heavy I could hardly move under them. In the mornings I had the joy of taking my calliper from under the bed and placing my left leg into it. It was like wearing ice. Any juvenile displays of impending manhood would be quickly banished as the top ring of the calliper reached my groin.

As the winter progressed my right leg became covered in chilblains. The doctor sent me to the local hospital, where I received the wise advice that I should try to keep warm. They had clearly never been to my home. They applied creams and bandages, but the sores remained until the spring.

In those days it was normal practice for people to clear the snow from the pavement in front of their own home, and most did so. This meant walking on pavements was relatively easy, although there was always a danger of slipping on ice. The weight of traffic cleared the main roads, but the side streets remained covered. What a joy when spring finally arrived and brought some sun with it.

When the plaster was removed from my right leg, I was informed that I did not need a full calliper on that leg and was given a short one that stopped below my knee. I also acquired a new calliper for my left leg. This had a joint in the middle, so when I sat down I could bend my leg. This was hugely advantageous, but it came with its own dangers. The first such joint was designed like a mortise and tenon joint, with the metal from the bottom of the calliper slotting into the middle of a gap in the upper part. A metal sleeve had to be pushed down to lock it or pulled to open it. If I did not ensure that the sleeves on both sides were firmly in position the calliper would give way the minute I tried to stand, leaving me in a heap on the floor. This mechanism was later replaced by a bar behind the knee that was easier to operate. The bar just had to be pulled upwards to release the lock and pushed down when the leg was straight to lock it. Again, great care had to be taken. There were many times when the simple manoeuvre was not performed correctly and I crashed to the floor. As I grew older these falls became heavier, more painful and more dangerous.

Living with my family gave me another perspective on life that I had not anticipated. As for most working-class families of the time, holidays meant no more than not going to school. Hardly anybody went away from home for what is now understood as a holiday. There was insufficient money for such luxuries and the most that people could expect would be a ferry ride from Liverpool to New Brighton, where there was a beach and a funfair. An exception might be a week in a caravan in North Wales.

However, when I was 11 or 12 the British Polio Fellowship (BPF) took an interest in me. In those days very few hotels had facilities for disabled people, and even people who could afford them were often unable to find an accessible hotel or boarding house where they could spend their money. A number of charities responded by opening their own holiday homes. The BPF had opened a hotel, the Lantern in Worthing. In its 1956 Annual Report it stated "From a national point of view the Lantern Hotel has two faults – it is too popular at peak periods and, for many of our northern and Scottish members, it is too far away." [3] Its answer was to buy a large house in Clifton Road, in Lytham St Anne's, near Blackpool. This was then converted to meet the needs of disabled people and became the Northern Lantern.

The BPF offered me and some other boys who had had polio a free holiday at the Northern Lantern. We were accompanied by a group of adults from the Merseyside branch, and spent time on the beach and visited Blackpool. I recall that one day we were given five shillings to spend in Woolworths, equivalent to almost £5 today. No wonder I felt so rich. Some years later my weekly wages were £5. These were simple holidays by the seaside with sand and buckets and spades, but they were too expensive for most people I knew.

One of the people I got to know through the BPF was Alastair Shaw, who had contracted polio as a young man. He earned his living as a stamp dealer

---

3. North Barry. The Bulletin. British Polio Fellowship, July 2011

but enjoyed fishing. To get him to the edge of his chosen river he drove a Land Rover, not the posh executive type but a tough hardy machine with canvas covering the back. That was where we boys sat, looking out through the rear which was open to the world. From that vantage point we could imagine any number of adventurous scenarios. Alastair remained a close friend until his death and was one of the many people who were always there to give me help and encouragement. I have been fortunate to have known so many such people.

Alastair was one of the people responsible for creating the Heswall Disabled Children's Holiday Fund, which from the early 60s arranged what became known as the Heswall Camp. Heswall is on the Wirral Peninsula, but it could have been in a foreign country as far as I was concerned. The first camp was held under canvas in the grounds of Calday Grammar School in 1961, but in 1962 it moved to the Heswall Boys Camp.[4] The site was owned by Liverpool Youth Association and had accommodation blocks, a games room and full catering facilities. It also had an open-air swimming pool in which the water was so cold it felt like going down with the *Titanic*. I entered it only once, discovered I could not breathe and was quickly lifted out.

---

4. A history of "the boys camp" Broad Lane, Heswall, The Heswall Society, June 2007.

Each year about 20 disabled boys would spend a week at the camp for which there was no charge. Because people connected with the BPF were the movers and shakers behind it, all the boys had personal experience of polio. This was later to change and boys with a wider range of impairments were included, and then girls joined the camp.

Of course, nothing is free. The use of the camp, the hiring of the charabanc and the cost of the places we visited all had to be paid for – but not by the boys or their families. The organisers had to raise funds for the camp, and I later discovered that in those days it was almost entirely funded by the people of Heswall.

The camp had a simple formula. We slept in dormitories and after breakfast, events or outings were arranged for the morning, afternoon and evening. They would include trips to North Wales, the funfair at New Brighton, Chester Zoo, the cinema, swimming, sports and so on. On one occasion in 1962 we were due to travel on the hovercraft from Moreton to Rhyl in North Wales. At the time this was the only passenger hovercraft in the world. We all travelled from the camp to Moreton in the battered charabanc, known as Linda, which was used as our main form of transport. Broad Lane, where the camp was located, was full of potholes, and whatever other charms Linda possessed, proper suspension was not among them. We all received a certificate for travelling on the world's first passenger hovercraft. It was a bit of a con, because although a regular service was supposed to be provided the hovercraft was notoriously unreliable and the service was often cancelled. So it was on the day we visited. We were however allowed to sit in the cockpit while the pilot showed us the controls.

A final word about Linda. She did not have a fitted lift and the only way we could get into it was to be carried by the volunteers, who must surely have needed a holiday when the camp ended.

All the staff who supported our annual holiday were volunteers. Some were from the Liverpool youth movement, others were university students and always in the background were Alastair and his Heswall friends. Alastair eventually became the Patron of the camp, and after his death in 2002 I was invited to become the new Patron. The camp has moved to new premises and now includes girls as well as boys. It is still run by volunteers (some of whom attended the camp as children), who each year raise about £25,000 to cover the costs. The children still visit Chester Zoo, but new activities have been added. In 2015 one started at Liverpool Airport, where the youngsters were assisted into small four-seater aircraft and flown around Merseyside.

Looking back, I realise a considerable amount of time and energy had been expended in organising this camp for us. We were taken on boat trips on the

River Dee and even spent a day on a dredger around Liverpool Bay as it sought to keep the shipping lanes deep enough for the ships. These activities simply weren't available to most people, and the fact that I was disabled was opening up opportunities and experiences that my brothers and sisters were denied.

The Merseyside branch of the BPF arranged a swimming session at the Garston Baths every Thursday night. Although it was a normal public pool, on a Thursday the water was heated to about 90 degrees Fahrenheit. This was in the south of Liverpool and it would have been difficult for me to get to. This problem was quickly resolved when the BPF arranged for a physiotherapist, Miss Joyce Williams, to provide a chauffeur service, which she did for many years. She was an organised woman and took no chances. Every five years her Mini Minor was changed for a new one. On one occasion she picked me up in her new car when it was just a few hours old. At a roundabout she braked gently, but the motorist behind still managed to run into her. I can imagine the language many people would have used. Her response was "Oh, botheration!"

It was only later I really appreciated how much time people with busy lives devoted to giving disabled kids a good start in life. My friends and I were certainly beneficiaries of their kindness. Miss Williams was not only my chauffeur for Thursday evenings but would also ensure I could attend the various swimming galas.

The Paralympics were in their infancy in the 1960s with the first Games having taken place in Rome in 1960. A complicated classification system of people's ability had to be developed so that they competed against others of similar ability. The BPF also wanted to ensure that everybody had an equal opportunity of winning. To achieve this, each competitor was timed at their local swimming sessions over a number of weeks, so it was known how long it took them to swim so many lengths using a particular stroke. There was, of course, a temptation to swim more slowly, but the assessors knew all the tricks and knew what the swimmers were capable of. The accuracy of their timings could be seen in the regional swimming galas. Backstroke was my fastest stroke, but even so I was hardly fast.

The slowest swimmers started first according to their speed. In a race of four lengths I often had to swim two lengths before the faster swimmers were allowed to enter the water. There was one boy from Preston who was often pitted against me and was a much stronger swimmer. He got medals and cups for winning and normally beat me. Sometimes I had more than two lengths start on him, but as I reached the end he was already waiting and would feign disgust and complain, "For God's sake, will you get a move on, I'm freezing here!" I got prizes for most improved performance or for trying. The classic trophies of a loser!

In addition to the swimming sessions, the BPF played an important part in my life. Polio is a disease that does not recognise wealth or social class, and one consequence was that many of the people supporting the local branch lived in the better-off parts of the city or in the suburbs beyond. These were people who raised money to fund the swimming sessions and other activities. I was therefore invited to attend garden parties, village fairs and other fundraising events in parts of Merseyside with which I was unfamiliar. I was amazed to see some of the houses in which these people lived. They seemed huge. They did not have a backyard but instead what seemed to be a small field that they called a 'garden'. The whole event could take place in the garden seemingly without anybody using the house in front of it. I would always be made very welcome. I was always encouraged to get on with life and not to let disability limit my ambitions. I'm not sure that I had ambitions at that time, but I was being exposed to another world.

Sometimes traditional charities, like the BPF, are criticised for being too limited in their expectations and not taking a larger role in campaigning or advocacy work. However, I found that through the local branch of this national charity I received constant support and friendship and was enabled to enjoy experiences that would otherwise have been beyond my reach. I have remained a member of the BPF all my life. In the 1990s I did become involved in campaigning but only to draw attention to what became known as Post Polio Syndrome, when it was discovered that people who had had polio decades before were experiencing new symptoms.

I had joined the Scouts at Greenbank and this had been a great source of pleasure and adventure. I saw no reason to stop attending when I left the school, although there was the problem of how to get to the weekly meetings, as public transport would have meant difficult bus journeys. The Scout leader, Ron McManus (Mac), soon found an answer. He had gradually expanded the troop so that a growing percentage were not pupils at Greenbank. He arranged for volunteer drivers to pick up boys at their home and to take them home again after the meetings. It was through this arrangement that I first met Bill Fothergill. I was told that somebody would collect me and at the agreed time Bill arrived in a huge car that was clearly almost new. It caused a sensation in the street.

Bill was tall with white hair and a white moustache. Most memorably he wore on his head a deerstalker hat similar to that worn by the fictional detective Sherlock Holmes. Inevitably, we boys gave him the nickname Sherlock, and so he became known. He was a sales director for a tool company and supplied equipment to factories such as car plants. Through him I learned what went on in factories and some of the poor working practices that would later contribute to the demise of the British car manufacturing industry. Sherlock and Mac lived close to each other and had met during their days in the Army.

Although the 17th Wavertree Scout Troop was classified as a troop for disabled scouts, that was not allowed to inhibit our activities. By this time in the paddock at Greenbank a wooden hut had appeared. This was the home of the 12th Wavertree, and a few joint activities were arranged. I soon discovered that there was nothing conventional about the 12th. They had Scottish links and wore kilts. The scouts were almost without exception exceedingly clever and seemed able to resolve any problem thrown at them. They could also see no reason why disabled boys should not do all the things they did. For example, at camp they would rig ropes between the trees and slide from one tree to another across the open ground beneath using a pulley. This aerial runway looked like dangerous fun, so the 12th created slings to haul the disabled boys up the tree and then secured us onto the pulley. Then with a strong shove, off we flew to the next tree. I suspect that today 1000 safety regulations would need to be met before anyone was allowed to behave with such freedom, but it was typical of the attitude of the 12th and some of the boys I met then remain close friends. Their leader, Spencer Legg, had a good relationship with Miss Long, and each year the 12th arranged a Christmas Party for the school. Some years later some of us would still meet with the 12th in their hut for parties that were not in the Scout Manual.

Getting ready for Scouts meant changing into the uniform. The neckerchief was held together at the front by a leather woggle. For some reason this went missing every week, so part of the ritual was me calling to Mum, "Mum, where's me woggle?" to which she would reply, "Where you left it", which was not a lot of help as I had clearly forgotten where I left it. When I resorted to "I've got to find it, Mum, Sherlock will be here soon", Mum would join the search and find it.

As I rose through the ranks and became a Patrol Leader I was given more responsibilities. At one camp held at Tawd Vale we were joined by a cub pack of blind boys. I was instructed to ensure they had a wash before breakfast. To this end I arranged for hot water in bowls to be provided. Naturally, they objected to getting washed at all while at camp, but they cooperated when I informed them sausage and beans would be ready as soon as they were washed. Superficial washing took place, and then to my surprise some of the boys took out their artificial eyes to wash them. Some let go of their eyes, which mingled with other eyes in water. I think that eventually I managed to restore the right eyes to the right boys, but it is still possible that some wore someone else's eyes for years afterwards!

Through my early teens I was therefore developing a life separate from that with my family and the community in Tweed Street, but much was also happening at home. Tweed Street was vibrant and there was usually something going on. Boys would be playing football, girls were using skipping ropes and others would be upside down standing on the hands with their feet against a wall and their dresses tucked into their knickers. There were a number of games based on the principles of hide and seek but involving hiding anywhere in the area. Some of the boys were racing around on steering carts, and I persuaded dad to make me one. A few planks and wheels from an old pram provided most of the raw material. I discovered that my younger brother Lenny, who was fast growing up, could run fast and was more than happy to push me on the steering cart in races. Such was his speed that mostly we won any race we entered. The steering cart, providing I could find a willing pusher, also meant I could go further than I could walk, and get there faster.

An important part of life were the matinees at the pictures on a Saturday afternoon. Cinemas surrounded us. At the top of the little entry was the Cosy, the local flea-pit. Joan would go to the Cosy with a pen and paper to write down the names of the films due to be shown, and Dad and Granddad would study the list to decide whether a film deserved their presence. There were the Palladium and the Royal, both within walking distance, but my favourite was the Casino, on Kensington about half a mile away. It was possible to pay with lemonade bottles as they had a value when returned to shops. There would always be the news by Pathé, a cartoon, a short film and then the main feature, which was often some branch of the US military winning the war single-handed or a bunch of cowboys sorting out Indians. Little did we know that Indian land was being stolen by the so-called good guys. But that was Saturdays.

Before I had left Greenbank, Dad had acquired an old boat. It was a 27-foot former lifeboat, or so he told me, and lived either in the water of Dukes Dock or on the quay. He named it *Girl Joan*, after my sister. It seemed to require a great deal of attention for its very occasional voyages into Liverpool Bay. Dad used to take me to the boat, where one of my jobs was to paint the hull with oil-based paint to stop water seeping between the planks. It seemed to leak regardless of how much paint was slapped onto it. I recall one occasion when we were sailing in the Mersey when I had to constantly pump the bilge to expel surplus water. I'm not sure what happened to *Girl Joan*, but suspect Dad let her rot in the dock when he tired of her. However, visiting the boat gave me an opportunity to see inside one of Liverpool's docks and all the hustle and the bustle of the dockers. It would not be too many years before most of the docks were bereft of ships and dockers as goods became containerised.

By now I could get around Liverpool using the buses. They were still difficult to get on and off, but the conductor would always help and I would stand under the stairs on the rear platform, as this meant I did not need to negotiate extra steps. I visited libraries and chose those where the bus stopped near the entrance. These were often a greater distance than local libraries, but the amount of walking required was significantly less because of bus routes. I would also visit friends around the city. Looking back I'm sure Mum would have had some anxiety about my travelling, but she never sought to prevent me. She would tell me not to read so much because I would wear out my eyes. She might have had a point, because in the house I normally had my head in a book or a comic. But with such a large family there was never much peace inside the house, with a constant stream of friends knocking for one person or another. I remain amazed that Mum managed to raise eight children and still held a part-time job at the local school.

Mum needed to work because money was unreliable. Even on those occasions when Dad earned good wages he would give Mum a very small amount of it on which to feed us all. The greater proportion was kept for himself. This really epitomised Dad's attitude to his family. He didn't do anything around the house and would have regarded all household duties as being "the wife's" duties. His role was to bring the money in. This also gave him ownership of the family, and he expected his instructions to be followed. In this sense he was an authoritarian king in his little kingdom. He had a sense of humour, and in circumstances in which employment was precarious he often found ways to keep at least some money flowing. But if Mum had not received the weekly Family Allowance, things would have been much tighter financially.

One of Dad's schemes was to sell firewood in local streets. He rented a small basement where he would use a circular saw to cut pieces of wood into strips about 6 inches long. I would then place a quantity in a shaped vice which forced them together into a tight bundle and then wrap a piece of wire around them. Now they were ready for sale at 3p bundle. When he had enough to fill his small battered van, he would knock on doors until he had sold them. The fact that we now had a TV and a van was a sign we were going up in the world!

His greatest challenge was when my two sisters and I reached an age when we wished to attend parties and stay out late. He would insist we return home at a set time, which was usually before the party was in full bloom. Naturally, we began to stretch his instructions or even ignore them. Georgina was particularly independently minded and was often the subject of a physical beating as his authority waned. He disapproved of Georgina's boyfriend and banned her from seeing him. Such draconian instructions were bound to be ignored. Although he was not in any way religious, he objected furiously to Joan's boyfriend on the basis that he was Catholic. Even years later he said he would not attend the wedding, and although he did, he wore a sour face all day.

Before I left school I had the final operation of my childhood at Fazakerley Hospital. Mr O'Malley, my consultant, asked to see my parents for permission to operate. It was given and so I entered hospital for several months. This time the plan was to move muscles to ensure my right hip joint did not dislocate. After pre-med I was taken to theatre, and when I woke up both legs were covered in plaster and a piece of wood across the bottom ensured the hip joints were immobile. To say this was uncomfortable would be an understatement. I was in agony, but all the nurses would say was "Don't be silly, it will soon feel better." I kept complaining and insisted the surgeon have a look.

I was told it was unnecessary, but I kept insisting and pointed out that my toes were an odd colour.

Eventually one of the surgeons, Mr T, arrived He was a jovial, cheerful man who said "Hello, sausage, what's the problem?" I'd had enough. I responded, "I'm not a bloody sausage. Someone has put the plaster on too tight." He took a look and agreed. The plaster was removed, but sadly it was then replaced. It was less painful but no less uncomfortable. When it was eventually removed it took another few months for me to learn to walk again, and until I could, I could not be discharged. This entire operation was a waste of time and money.

By this time I had developed a deep suspicion about the necessity for many of the medical interventions to which disabled kids were subject. Some of the operations seemed experimental and others unnecessary. There is a price a disabled child pays for time in hospitals that is measured in lost schooling and the opportunities forgone. There is also a cost to their families in visiting hospitals etc. In those days medical opinion overruled all, but the medics saw only one aspect of a child's life. At the age of 16 I got my mother to agree that she would not give consent for any more operations.

I soon learnt how to cope in this ward. It had been an isolation ward, so we all had our small room. It was run not by the nurses but by the cleaner, Agnes, who had been there for a million years. It was Agnes who ensured people were fed and had cups of tea as well as repelling bugs and infections. If a patient had no visitors Agnes would arrive in her own time to play cards with them. She was the heart and soul of the ward.

One of the patients was Dave, who had a brain injury after being hit by a cricket ball. He used a wheelchair and had limited use of his arms. Everything he did was slow, so he earned the nickname "Flash". One skill Flash had was picking horses, and he introduced me to gambling. I would pick a horse with his advice and Agnes would place the bets. As we won more than we lost, we could maintain this until we were discharged.

The end of schooldays were approaching and Alastair Shaw appeared at our home and asked Mum if she would mind if I went to Spain for two weeks with the Wallasey Disabled Persons Swimming Club, in which Alastair was a leading light. The downside was it would cost £60, a huge sum of money for Mum. It was agreed it could be paid in instalments of about £5. After about £20 had been paid Alastair re-appeared to inform mum that an anonymous donor had paid the balance, and so I had my first overseas holiday at a time before the inclusive holiday package industry had taken off. We flew from Manchester Airport in a DC9 that flew through a thunderstorm, so it rocked and heaved. It was adventure after adventure. In those days airlines seemed much more relaxed about disabled passengers than they were to become some decades later.

As I approached the age of 16 my schooldays were drawing to an end. There was no question that I would have to get a job, but what job? In those days careers advice was provided to schools and their pupils by the local education authority through what was known as the Youth Employment Bureau, and one of their staff specialised in the pupils at special schools. Her name was Miss Barbara Lester. When I first met her she seemed old and severe, but I soon discovered she was good at her job and determined to get us into the workforce one way or another. Although very few pupils left special schools with academic qualifications, there were employment opportunities, because Liverpool still possessed a number of factories that offered low-skilled employment. Instead of making a decision about my employment prospects, Miss Lester decided the best way forward would be for me to have a full employment assessment. When I left school I was therefore sent to an Industrial Rehabilitation Unit for a six-week assessment. And so began another chapter.

Chapter 4

Beyond School

Just after I left school, I received through the post a
green card from the Department of Employment and
Productivity. It informed me that I was now registered
as disabled under the provisions of the Disabled
Persons (Employment) Act 1944. I was later to learn
that this gave me special access to jobs such as
lift operator and car park attendant, as these jobs
were reserved for disabled people. It also meant that
employers of more than 20 people could include me
towards the 3% quota of disabled people that they
were meant to employ. At the time it all meant nothing
to me. I was leaving school with no job to go to and

seemingly no hope of getting one. But Barbara Lester was not to be defeated so easily.

Following a conversation and a few tests in her office, at which I had apparently performed rather badly, or at least slowly, in picking up individual pins from a table, I think she concluded that manual work was not for me. Happily, in those days there were plenty of low-level office jobs, but it seemed I was also unqualified for these. Her solution was to enrol me in the local Industrial Rehabilitation Unit. IRUs were normally attached to Government Training Centres where building skills, bricklaying, car mechanics and such trades were taught.

A few weeks after leaving school I started a six-week assessment course at the IRU, in Aintree. Despite its name, the purpose of the IRU was not to rehabilitate but to assess whether a person was employable, and if so, for what type of job. Finally, it would make recommendations on training. It was far from a perfect system, but 50 years later I witnessed the distress caused to many disabled people whose social security benefits were cut because, on the basis of a short interview, an assessor of limited expertise decided whether the person was capable of holding down a job. Inevitably, professional standards and accuracy of assessments were seen as less important than reducing the social security benefits bill. The assessors were under pressure to find that people were "fit for work". As a consequence, some people who had been judged fit to work died within a week of the assessment. Yet for all its faults, the assessment system in the 1960s was far advanced compared with that after 2010.

At the time I did not understand how the IRU operated, but Mary Greaves described it in her report "Work and Disability".[5] Rehabilitation was seen as having three distinct elements. The first was medical rehabilitation aimed at restoring function after an accident or illness. Social rehabilitation was aimed at helping people to integrate into the community and to live at home. In between was vocational rehabilitation, designed to equip people with the skills employers were seeking. The IRU was often the first stage of vocational rehabilitation. The various courses were planned and controlled by the Unit Case Conference, comprising the rehabilitation officer, medical officer, occupational psychologist, social worker, the chief occupational supervisor and the disablement resettlement officer. Collectively this was a skilled team of people who knew something of industry and commerce as well as techniques for assessing disabled people.

On my first day I was struck by how rundown the IRU appeared to be, but apparently this was deliberate

5. Greaves, Mary, Work and Disability, British Council for Rehabilitation of the Disabled, 1969

policy as it wished to emulate a modern factory. After several staff had interviewed me I was asked to perform my first work task. I was given a hacksaw and instructed to cut a gallon petrol tin in half. As an overconfident 16-year-old I wasted no time in pointing out that it would take me ages to complete the task and I would never be able to do a job, in the unlikely event one was offered, involving sawing tins into two pieces. Anyway, I pointed out "if you want to cut tin cans in half you would use a circular saw and not a hacksaw. It will be much more efficient and safer." Knowing about cutting firewood, which I had watched my Dad do, was obviously an advantage!

The staff were unfazed and found other ways to test my physical dexterity. I was placed in the office studies section, where I was taught basic bookkeeping. This resembled a 1950s school classroom rather than an office, but it served its purpose.

Most of the other trainees were much older than me and had already worked in a number of places. They were helpful in guiding me and also in ensuring I learned the important rules. No work at all was to be done during the one-hour lunch break, as this was sacrosanct. At least once or twice a week we would cross the road outside the Unit and have a liquid lunch in the pub. I learned as much from my fellow trainees as I did from the formal sessions. I suspect even this was planned, as the wide age group mixed freely.

It was a difficult journey by public transport to the IRU, but the return journey was sometimes easier because Dad would arrive on a scooter to give me a lift home. My elbow crutches were tucked inside his belt while I sat behind clinging on.

Eventually, my assessment was complete and it was decided that I could do office-based work but currently lacked the knowledge to do so. It was therefore recommended that I attend a residential training college for disabled people. Although there were five such colleges in England, there were none in the North West. The nearest was Portland College just outside Mansfield in Nottinghamshire. Before I could attend Portland I needed to pass the entrance exam. Apparently it was easy, but I still managed to fail.

However Barbara Lester was not giving up yet. I was called to see her in her office. She pointed out that I had not failed the exam by much, but it was understood by everybody that I had missed a great deal of my schooling because of medical appointments and lengthy stays in hospital. She suggested I should do a further education course before applying for the office skills course. Portland offered such a course and Lester wanted me to attend it. There were no suitable facilities in Liverpool, so the course at Portland seemed to be a reasonable way forward. It was many years later that I realised Liverpool City Council had met the cost of my accommodation and education at Portland until I qualified for the vocational course, which was funded by central government. Despite this, Portland, as a charity, was always seeking to raise funds for new buildings or facilities. Years later I had to fight for people to be able to attend these courses as local authorities and government looked for less-expensive provision. In the 1960s, however, I was never made to feel cost was an issue. The City Council was keen to follow what was considered to be best practice. In the 1960s discrimination against disabled people was rife and campaigns to put that right came later. Nonetheless local and national government were happy to spend money to enable disabled people to earn their living, and provided the resources for us to do so.

Miss Lester completed the application form and I signed as instructed. She then said, "There is, of course, a six-month waiting list. I will contact you as soon as there is a vacancy." The delay horrified me. "What do I do for money until then?" I asked. "Well, you are entitled to social security," she said. In those days the unemployment pay system was strongly linked to the contributions a person had paid in the past. I had no contribution history and therefore the amount of money I received would be only just sufficient to keep body and soul in the same place. Not an enticing prospect!

"Do you have any jobs at all on your books that I could do?" I asked.

"Well", she said, "there is a vacancy for a lift operator in Water Street. Would you be interested? The wages are £5 a week." From my point of view, it was a job and I grabbed it.

An interview was arranged with the caretaker, Ray, of a building in Water Street, which was part of the commercial heart of the city centre. He was a larger-than-life figure who was also disabled, having one arm with limited function, but he lived life to the full and was inspirational. Ray guided me down a corridor that led from the front to the back of the building. At the end was my new kingdom: the lift. It was probably as old as the building itself. It had two metal gates that I had to open and close. Movement was controlled by a lever which was pressed forward for up and pulled backwards for down. My job, I was informed, was to ensure it stopped level with each floor so people did not trip when entering or leaving. There was a small tip-up seat that I could sit on. There seemed to be no heating in this part of the building and I was advised to wear something warm.

A few months later, when winter arrived, it was very cold. With Ray's agreement I visited the agents who managed the building and asked them if I could have a heater near the lift. I felt like Oliver Twist asking for more. The agents' offices were fully carpeted and warm. I suspected they did not know what the word cold meant. I was told they would think about it, and a few weeks later a small and ineffective heater arrived.

After a few weeks I had learnt about all there was to learn about driving a lift in one of two directions. The building was occupied by small companies, some of which had rigid rules. There were, from memory, five or six floors, but the only way people in the front half of the building could reach the back half was via a corridor on the ground floor. At the top of the back of the building were located the ladies' toilets. I thus had a rush of women between 10.30 and 11 each day and then few if any customers until lunchtime. I soon got to know the people in the different companies and they looked after me, ensuring I had a steady supply of reading material. In what would otherwise have been a boring job the people who worked in the building ensured most days contained some colour.

I was increasingly conscious that there were several hours a day when I really had nothing to do. There was a small disused office very close to the lift and I asked Ray if I could use it. Understandably, he wanted to know the reason, so I told him "a friend has suggested I could make a few bob printing personal notepaper. I could buy a second-hand Adana printing machine through Exchange & Mart magazine and then all I would need would be a few fonts and some paper."

Somewhat bemused by this ludicrous idea, he agreed, but pointed out that I still needed to respond to the bell in the lift and that if I heard people walking down the cavernous corridor I had to get back to the lift so they were not kept waiting.

I approached a number of printers in Liverpool to see if they had any old fonts they could sell me cheaply (this was in the days when printing had to be done using the hot metal process in which the letters are stamped by rows of moulded characters arranged by a compositor). Invariably they had shelves of fonts they no longer used that they were happy to give to me free of charge. One printer told me he also had a large supply of notepaper from the days when he printed personal stationery, but now he concentrated on larger orders. "You might as well have it all", he said and so with hardly any outlay I was ready for business. I took orders at church garden fetes or the gatherings of the British Polio Fellowship. I proposed to charge them half a crown for every order I took. The income never reached £5 a week, but it was a useful addition to my wages.

Like many boys in the 1950s and 60s I had spent some years collecting stamps. My friend Alastair Shaw was a professional philatelist and stamp dealer and provided encouragement. I realised that most boys collected colourful stamps and that these were often the least expensive. Retail prices were contained in the Stanley Gibbons catalogue and the lowest price was normally about 2p, whereas through Alastair I could buy hundreds for a few shillings. Selling them at a fraction of the Gibbons price would be profitable. I discussed the idea with Sherlock, who thought it might work and asked me to work out what stationery would be required. Once he had this information he provided it all. This enterprise was not a great success because of the low prices needed to generate high volumes to make it all worthwhile, but it was another attempt to top up my wages.

There was a barbershop near the building and behind it was a café which sold a cooked lunch and a mug of tea for 1/6d (7½p), but one day I was to dine in much greater grandeur. I was walking down a side street towards the building in which I worked when I placed my elbow crutch on a metal grid that was part of the pavement. The grid gave way and my crutch disappeared into a drainpipe. Naturally, I fell over and as people rushed to help me to my feet an elderly lady ran over and said, "Sue them, that shouldn't happen. Sue them!" I wasn't sure whom I should sue or why, but then a smartly-dressed man appeared and said, "I'm sorry about the drain. We will get it fixed, but if you come back at lunchtime you can have a free meal". It was only at this point I realised I was outside a smart restaurant. I was not accustomed to eating in such places, as the café behind the barbershop was much more my style. But the offer of a free meal is not to be ignored, and so I presented myself at lunchtime for my free meal. I was of course completely out of place. I was the only person dining alone and the only person not wearing a suit. Who would have thought that being a liftboy could involve so much drama and adventure?

While I was at the IRU I received a letter inviting me to attend a clinic at Mill Road Hospital. Most people in Liverpool thought of Mill Road as a maternity hospital and it was where most of my brothers and sisters were born. It also housed the Artificial Limb and Appliance Centre, ALAC. There were ALAC centres throughout the country. I was to be assessed on whether I could safely drive an invalid tricycle. A man known as the Technical Officer, or TO, carried out the assessment, and his decision was final. The trike was a small single-seat vehicle that had a door on the left side. At the back there were two wheels and at the front a single wheel. I demonstrated that I could open the door and position myself on the seat. There was no steering wheel but instead a lever that looked as though it had been stolen from a motorbike. This was connected to the trike on the right-hand side and was positioned in front of me. I was instructed that to turn right I should push it forward and to turn left I should pull it towards me. To brake I should push it down. The trike was located in what appeared to be an old Nightingale-type ward from which all beds had been removed.

The TO said "I'm going to push you down the ward. When I say "brake" I want you to brake as hard and fast as you can." I did so. I was then informed that I qualified, but first a few details needed to be sorted out.

Although the body of the trike was fibreglass and would not rust, the Ministry of Health required people to have a garage in which to keep it. If they did not have a garage but had space for one, the Ministry would supply a pre-made one. This was a problem for me, because I lived in a small terrace house that had been built before the motorcar was invented. However, in the street there was one house that did possess what could pass as a garage. It belonged to the Dolmans, who owned a chandler's shop on Boaler Street. They had always been kind to me, so I put my problem to them. Mr Dolman said, "That's not a problem. Tell the hospital people you can park it in my garage and I'll sign a bit of paper agreeing." We both knew my new machine would be parked outside my front door and would never see the garage, but the boxes could be ticked and some weeks later my trike arrived. It was pale blue with a white roof and the registration number was NTW 555C.

I was not allowed to use it until the Institute of Advanced Motorists had given me driving lessons. This was something of an experience, because there was only one seat. Between the seat and the door was a flip-down transfer board to help the driver get to the seat. The large instructor sat on the transfer board alongside the seat, thus giving me some comfort that my friends could do the same and I could ignore the instruction under the speedometer "Passenger carrying is strictly forbidden". He did emphasise that this was exceptional and I should not carry passengers because it would invalidate the insurance. Once he regarded me as competent, I was free to drive on a provisional licence.

I now had my own car, paid for by the government, which maintained, taxed and insured it, and once a year sent me a cheque towards the cost of fuel. The cheque was not a lot even then, but in the mid-sixties three gallons of petrol cost less than £1.00. The government never referred to the trike as a car but always as an 'invalid tricycle'. Users normally referred to them as Noddy cars, although Noddy had passenger seats in his car. The trike had many names, but for the sake of consistency I refer to them as Invacars. A purist would point out that the Invacar was but one model and there were also the AC, the Tippen and the Barratt, which were all different. They would be right but they all operated in the same way and the one I used was an Invacar.

I was soon to discover the many disadvantages of the Invacar, but now at the age of 16 I had a set of wheels that offered endless possibilities. Joe, my friend from Greenbank, had acquired his a year or so earlier and we decided we should join up for some camping in the Lake District. For our first trips we borrowed tents from the scouts, but they were difficult to erect. We decide to buy a tent with a sown-in ground sheet that was easier to erect. This cost £34 and meant we both had to get our fathers to act as guarantor for the debt of £17 each. This, of course, was long before the days of credit cards and all credit was strictly controlled. Although the tent was easier to erect, we found the fastest way to get it up was to peg out the bottom and look helpless. Other campers would always offer to help and the tent was up in minutes.

My agreeable life as an Invacar-driving liftboy was now to come to an end. There was a place waiting for me at Portland College, so I resigned my job, said goodbye to the many people I had met in my lift and took my printing equipment home, where Mum helped me pack for Portland. I had already discovered two of the attributes of the Invacar. One was that the engine was only 197cc and was being asked to carry more weight than it was designed for. It was thus underpowered and had a maximum speed of about 40-45 miles an hour. The second was that it did not have a heater, and there were so many gaps in the structure that there was a constant flow of cold air. So heavy coats and a blanket were needed in the winter for long journeys.

Portland was over 100 miles away. I became very familiar with the route: Liverpool to Warrington, Macclesfield, Buxton, Chesterfield, Mansfield. The scariest part was the road between Macclesfield and Buxton. The road atlas records this as the A537, but everyone knows it as the Cat and Fiddle, after the pub at its peak. From Macclesfield the road took a turn towards the sky as it climbed over the Pennines through the Peak District National Park. Even in summer the Invacar did not like these hills, and it liked them even less in the winter. At full power I could sometimes reach 20 miles an hour uphill, but I was often down to 15. On the narrow road there was soon a queue of lorries and cars behind me. It would be many years before the M62 was built to allow this traffic to speed across the Pennines. Now we were all stuck on one of the three main routes across the hills. As soon as there was a layby I would pull over, much to the relief of the drivers anxious to get past me. It did raise doubts in my mind about whether these Invacars were fit for purpose, but that battle would wait for another day.

When I arrived at Portland I turned left into a long driveway, at the end of which was the reception area to which I reported. I was shown to the four-bed dormitory. The men's accommodation blocks were near the entrance and the single block for women was at the other end of the site. On the right was the recreation hall, and opposite to it was the refectory. The teaching blocks were scattered around the site, but the education section was near the refectory. On the first day Mr Geary, who seemed to be the person responsible for us, gathered us for a pep talk.

He recited his list of rules. "I don't want to see boys holding hands with girls" he said. This immediately prompted questions "Well, can we hold hands with other boys?" He was not amused. He was clearly an ex-army man and expected to be obeyed.

There were also strict rules about how late we could stay out, and if we were to stay out beyond that we needed a pass. We also needed a pass if we wanted to go home for a weekend. Geary was the first there to criticise my accent, which was broad Scouse. I could not see his problem. A Scouse accent in the mid-1960s with the Beatles at the top of all the charts could be advantageous.

My first clash with Geary was a couple of weeks later when I applied for a weekend pass to join friends in Liverpool who were planning a weekend of sin and debauchery that was not to be missed. Geary said I had not been there long enough and he would have to consult my parents, but there was not time to do so. I pointed out that this was his problem because I intended to go, pass or no pass. At the last moment the pass was produced. After that we got on better.

This military background to the college was not a

coincidence. It was founded after World War II to help get injured soldiers back to work and to help those who became disabled following accidents in the pits. After the war the major industry was coal mining and there was still a thriving mining community when I was there. It was built in the heart of Sherwood Forest on land that had been donated by the Duchess of Portland, whose picture hung in one of the smarter rooms that were part of the recreation block

Most of the college was concerned with vocational training, which ranged from gardening, handy for keeping the extensive grounds in order, to watchmaking. The training was of a high standard and most students got jobs when they left. The college had good links with local industry and this provided a plentiful supply of vacancies.

There was also a sheltered workshop that employed people who were unable to work to the levels required in factories and offices. They earned a full wage, but it was subsidised by the Employment Department. It manufactured tourist products under the branding of "Heart of Sherwood", because products that could be linked in even the slightest way with Robin Hood were sold in tourist outlets.

The education section was much smaller and there were about 20 students. The main teacher was a man who seemed elderly and drove a bright yellow DAF 33. Whatever his taste in car colours, he was a superb teacher who worked hard and worked his class equally hard. His name was Mr Parker, and he introduced me to Shakespeare and a host of poets of whom I had never heard. Every day was a new adventure with this man. Was education supposed to be fun? Mr Parker's task was to get us through the examination to enter a vocational course and at the end of six months we had far more education, knowledge and wild ideas than to merely pass the exam. He had woken us up!

Thus qualified, I was transferred to the Business Studies course. This had some important implications. The first was that we were paid a training allowance that was linked to wages in industry. As an education student, my local authority paid for my accommodation and the course fees. Social Security offered a small weekly payment for incidental expenses, such as clothes, on the basis that all other costs were covered. Thus I was paid one pound five shillings a week (£1.25p). There were ways of extracting additional funds from the Social by seeking special grants on the grounds that being disabled was expensive. Clothes wore out more quickly. Callipers ripped our trousers or skirts. We soon learnt all the tricks to increase our tiny income.

The food served in the refectory defies description and often tasted terrible, but it was no use complaining, as we would just be informed it was much better that that served in the army. This meant that the fish and chip shop four miles away in Mansfield was popular with those of us able to get to it. I reasoned that there was an opportunity here. If I offered to fetch fish and chip for 10 or more people I might get a discount from the chippy. In fact I did get a small discount, as well as a free portion of fish and chips. Through one scam or another I managed to survive the financial restrictions that accompanied the education course.

Being located in the heart of Nottinghamshire and having transport gave me an ideal opportunity to explore the local area. Lord Byron's former home, Newstead Abbey, was about a mile away, and in good weather provided a perfect retreat. The town of Mansfield did not appear to have made any special arrangements for disabled people but was obviously accustomed to students from Portland. If a small group of us visited the cinema, the staff made us welcome. There was no attempt to stop us going into cafés or pubs. Mansfield was a mining town and you took it as you found it. In the pubs it was difficult not to meet miners and it was not long before I was invited to some of their homes and the local social clubs. My abiding memory is of the generosity and hospitality of the small mining communities in Nottinghamshire.

The instructions we had received on our first day aimed at limiting sexual relationships were treated with the disrespect they deserved. The college was surrounded by an infinite number of discreet places for courtship, but first we needed to leave the college. This meant that the instruction in my Invacar "passenger carrying is strictly forbidden" had to be strictly ignored. I soon discovered that if I stayed within the county of Nottinghamshire the police were so accustomed to Invacar drivers carrying passengers that they turned a blind eye to it. But if I drove into the city of Nottingham, which had a separate police force, they would stop me and read the Riot Act. They expected the person I was with to get out and make progress using public transport. Once satisfied that I no longer had a passenger the police would drive away, and a few minutes later my passenger would re-join me.

There was one occasion when the county police were especially helpful. My passenger was a female student and we had parked near woodland in a high position from which no one could see into the Invacar but we had views of anything approaching. A police car turned off the main road onto the dirt track that led to our location. Fortunately, we had time to make ourselves presentable by the time the police car stopped in front of the Invacar. It could have been a scene from Pinewood Studios. The policeman was rotund and sported a full Jimmy Edwards moustache. I slid open the window and he peered in. "Is everything all right?" he asked. When I confirmed it was, he said, "That's fine then. I'll be passing this way again in 45 minutes or so, so flash your lights if there are any problems." That's the sort of copper I like!

Most of the blokes with whom I mixed were football fans but, like me, supported their local teams. Mine was Liverpool but others supported Manchester United, Stoke City, Burnley and so it went on. However, the local club, Mansfield Town, had reasonable access facilities, so when they were playing at home several of us went to watch them. On alternate weeks we would go to Nottingham Forest. It was a good time to watch them as one year they had a successful season and finished third in the old First Division.

Work also had to be done, and we were welcomed to the Business Studies Course on the first day by the tutor, Mr Humphries, who was himself disabled. He explained he had first attended Portland as a student, had worked for commercial companies and eventually returned as a tutor. The implication was clear: we were expected to achieve. He asked each of us to say something about ourselves. One person said his father was an accountant and Mr Humphries nodded his approval, saying, "You should have a start with bookkeeping". The student then said his father was a different sort of accountant: "He was a turf accountant."

We had six months to master the commercial world: the difference between public and private companies and partnerships, how to write business letters, bookkeeping skills up to trial balance. While we learned the skills, Humphries would patiently walk up and down the classroom leaning on his walking stick. At the end of the six months I was able to leave with a handful of certificates from the Royal Society of Arts officially attesting to my competence.

Although I was to leave the college, I still kept in touch with many of the friends I had made there. One was a young woman from Chesterfield, Pat, whose parents and brother always made me very welcome in their home. Her father, Mr Johnson, was a piano tuner and toured all around Derbyshire and Nottinghamshire. There didn't seem to be a part of the area he did not know intimately. Some years later I was staying with Pat for a weekend but on the Monday I needed to be back in Liverpool as I was starting a new job. Early on Sunday afternoon it started snowing and Mr Johnson informed me that the Cat and Fiddle was closed. I suggested I should go immediately and try the Snake, another well-named road that crossed the Pennines. He made a few phone calls and discovered that was also closed. A road further south was open but was expected to close. Not turning up for my first job was hardly the best start, but there did not seem to be too many options.

Mr Johnson then said, "Let's see what British Railways can do". He made a number of phone calls to British Railways in Sheffield, and then in his car he guided me and my Invacar to a rail freight yard in Sheffield, and it was loaded into one of the freight carriages. From there it was shunted to the passenger station and put on the end of a passenger train going to Manchester. I travelled on the train with it. At Manchester the Invacar was unloaded, and while this was happening the BR staff arranged a sandwich and a cup of tea for me. Then I was told my car was ready, but when I rejoined the Invacar I was surprised to see a police car. The police officer said "We don't know how well you know Manchester, but if we get you to the East Lancashire Road it will take you to Liverpool." And that is what happened. There was of course a cost. My ticket cost 23 shillings (£1.15). Moving the Invacar was charged at half that. Can you imagine trying to get such a service today?

Travelling between Mansfield and Liverpool also taught me more about the limitations of the Invacar. It would break down on many of the journeys. Some of these problems were easily solved. It had a two-stroke engine and only one spark plug, so if the cap came off, the vehicle would stop. It was simply a case of replacing it. On other occasions the plug would oil up and needed cleaning. This took a few minutes but was not a major problem.

More problematic was when the drive chain (similar to those on a motor-bike) snapped. There was no way I could repair this, but usually within half an hour a motor cyclist would stop, identify the problem and repair the chain. It seemed that in the North Midlands there was an endless supply of motorcyclists cruising around looking for disabled drivers to rescue. It could be argued that the distinct shape and colour of the Invacar was discriminatory, but the advantage was that if it broke down it did not take too long for someone to stop.

A more serious problem was a flat tyre. The Invacar did not have a spare wheel, so a new wheel had to be arranged. This was done by contacting the "Approved Repairer" in Liverpool or Wallasey and they would dispatch a driver with a spare wheel. For repairs that could not be done at the roadside, a spare vehicle was brought to replace the broken one and the original placed on a trailer and taken to Liverpool. This was a very expensive service, as there were approved repairers in all parts of the country but there seemed to be no way of using one nearby unless the driver lived in the area. I suspect part of the problem was that the Department of Health saw the Invacar as a type of wheelchair and did not envisage the wider use that was being made of them. It was the same line of thinking that ensured they were not fitted with a heater or even a basic radio. In fairness few cars had radios then, and because the two-stroke engine in the Invacar was so noisy, I doubt it would have been possible to hear a radio. The Invacar was intended to be functional.

There were no mobile phones of course, and if I was to contact the approved repairer, it meant a phone call. I would stop at the first house I reached and ask if I could use their phone. They almost always agreed, but when the problem became clear and I told them I would have to wait up to three hours for a replacement Invacar, some of these families asked me to join them for meals and to wait with them for as long as necessary. One of the upsides of being disabled is that we can see humanity at its wonderful best as well as seeing its more disagreeable face.

Despite the many problems with the Invacars, it would be misleading not to acknowledge that they gave us an enormous amount of freedom that we would otherwise have been denied. Joe and I toured much of the country driving in convoy with other friends. They were also a constant source of adventure as we tested their limitations. The rule that forbade passenger carrying was ignored, but carrying a passenger and a wheelchair was a problem. The only possible place for the wheelchair was in front of the tiller bar, but this restricted the space to push it forward to turn right, so only sweeping right turns could be made. More critically, if the chair jammed under the tiller, it was impossible to apply the brakes, but some still took this chance, including Joe, who once turned over his Invacar because it was the only way to stop it.

The light frame enabled them to skip over snow and

not sink into the ground on muddy fields. We could take our Invacars almost anywhere, and because their shape was so distinctive few objected when we did.

The police often turned a blind eye if we broke minor laws. On one occasion Joe was behind me at a roundabout in the Lake District and anticipated that I would spot a gap in the traffic and move. I failed to do so, but Joe moved to occupy what in his mind should have been a vacant space. All this was witnessed by a police officer, who just covered his face with his hands and walked away.

Chapter 5

Early Jobs

In 1967 I returned to my small family home in Liverpool. It had become more crowded as the family had grown. Dad was trying to assert his authority, but with less success as my sisters and I were resisting his self-imposed rules. Some things don't change. But others had to. I needed to get a job.

The first job I took, or rather seemed to fall into, was with a company called Display. The name was clearly intended to mislead people into thinking that it was connected to Remploy, which employed disabled people in factories throughout the country in sheltered conditions. Remploy was heavily subsidised by the government.

At Disploy I was expected to telephone companies and sell them advertising in one of a number of magazines that Disploy produced for charities. The emphasis was to be laid on the important work the charities were doing and the fact that Disploy employed disabled people, which was true, but there were only a handful of us. This seemed rather like begging, and I took an instant dislike to it. I stayed a few weeks and started looking for another job. In fairness to Disploy, what they were doing was the same as many other companies at the time. The business model was to agree with a charity that the company would produce a brochure, newsletter, magazine or other printed material free of charge. This not only freed the charity of the cost but also of the risk. In exchange, the company would sell advertising to be placed in the publication. Sometimes such advertising was purely commercial, but mostly it represented a way for companies to make a small donation to the charity and receive some publicity in the form of the advertisement. The advertisers invariably thought that the contribution would go to the charity, but instead it went to the publisher. A number of charities became wise to this and published their own journals and employed their own staff to sell the advertising.

Finding work in 1960s Liverpool was not too difficult, as the city was still vibrant. I knew that if I wrote for an interview in response to an advertisement, I was bound to be unsuccessful because my handwriting was so poor. But as ever, help was on hand. At the Labour exchange there was an official known as the Disablement Resettlement Officer (DRO), whose duties included assisting disabled adults to get work. Some disabled people I knew at the time thought they could sit back and the DRO would do all the work for them. This was completely unrealistic, but I found that by working with the DRO he could be extremely helpful. I scoured the *Liverpool Echo* for vacancies and when I found one that might be suitable I would drive to the Labour exchange and show the DRO the advertisement. If he agreed the job was possible, he would telephone the employer and arrange an interview for me.

The first job I was offered was with a company trading as the Army & Navy Stores that had a number of stores in the North West. I was employed in Liverpool city centre. The building still stands, but since then it has never found tenants to draw the crowds as the Army & Navy Stores did. The person clearly in charge was Miss Coates, who I discovered was a very sharp businesswoman and a superb buyer. Virtually all the goods she sold were excellent value for money, yet she bought them for a fraction of the cost for which she sold them.

These were the days before credit cards, and

almost all purchases were cash. Instead of having tills, the shop assistants would put the customer's money into a small-tubed canister. This was then placed into one of the pipes behind the counter. It would then be sucked to the top floor and emerge in front of the cashier. That was me. When a canister arrived, I would remove the cash and divide it into the appropriate drawers, immediately returning the canister to the shop assistant. If change was required, I supplied it. Not a difficult job until nine canisters arrived at once so someone had to wait. That would lead to a phone call from the shop assistant complaining that the customer was growing impatient. The phone call of course delayed me further. The biggest sin was to provide the wrong amount of change. That would almost always result in angry shop staff calling me all sorts of names. They soon calmed down.

The store manager was Miss Coates' son. Highly conscious of his own importance to the store and the world in general, he was a man of habit. Every Monday he would wear the same suit, then a different one on Tuesday and so on through the week. It was possible to identify the day of the week by the colour of the suit. He was in my office when the phone call that ended my short career occurred. One of the sales staff told me he had a Russian customer who wanted to pay in Norwegian Ores. Normally, this involved a phone call to the bank to get the exchange rate and then add a pound or so for the effort, to take account of the cost of converting and give a price in sterling. The man of suits listened in and suggested a price and then left. I still phoned the bank and the price I charged still covered all our costs and more. Half and hour later Suit Man arrived to ask why I had phoned the bank when he had given a price. I replied that I always checked as to guess could result in over or undercharging. The implication was that he was grossly overcharging, although it was not for me to voice the allegation.

The next day Miss Coates met me when I arrived for work. She had a packet containing a week's wages and told me to go home and not return. Suit Man had to be protected. Years later, when she retired or died, the stores began to decline and eventually closed. This is a pity because they were good stores, but I suspect Suit Man, who was nowhere near as bright as his mother, also lacked her business nous.

In 1960s Liverpool, red wagons bearing the name William Rainford Ltd were a common sight. I applied for, and was given, a job as a cost clerk. The fleet of vehicles must have been over 200 strong and they came in a variety of shapes. There were huge tipper trucks that would collect the remnants of the coal used at local power stations. This was known as 'aggregate' and had a number of uses, including being turned into breezeblocks for the building industry. They had a huge yard to accommodate what seemed like a city of breezeblocks. Other lorries were used to transport goods on behalf of other customers. The secret to making a profit was to ensure that somebody was also paying for the return journey, which meant significant work in ensuring the trucks did not travel empty. The building trade requires endless supplies of cement, and the fleet included vehicles with massive drums on the back for mixing it. The fleet was in two parts. Rainford owned part of it, with the remainder being owned by drivers who did contract work for them. Keeping this fleet on the road was a task in itself, so we had our own garage to do maintenance and repairs. It was important that the costs of spare parts that were fitted were invoiced to the right people, and as every invoice would be scrutinised they had to be accurate.

That was where I came in. I received a list of all the parts used. Mostly, it was a list of reference numbers. From the vehicle's registration number I would know which company had made it. From their catalogues and price lists, I would list the price we had been charged for the parts and if it was an owner-driver an extra percentage would be added to the cost. There were three of us doing costings. As I settled into the job I became involved in costing some of the demolition work which was another area of Rainford's work. As far as I can tell, our demolition work was highly regarded. Less so our civil engineering section.

On a day-to-day basis the company seem to be run by a rather miserable looking company secretary. I would see him prowling around the office from time to time, but he did not bother to speak to me, as I was far too junior to justify his attention. Two of the Rainford brothers, who had shares in the company, were there most days using their contacts to get contracts. About every week or so a man known as Mr William would appear. He arrived in a Rolls Royce and was always immaculately dressed. He spent most of his time in meetings of which I knew nothing, but he would also wander around the office and sometimes stopped at my desk to ask how things were going. They were short conversations, but at least he had style.

While its founder, Mr William, was alive the company seemed to thrive, even though he spent most of his time on his farms. The staff were typical Liverpudlians and were always having fun even when working hard. There was no canteen, but we had access to the one in the adjacent company, for which Rainfords paid.

I enjoyed my time there until the company secretary said he was unhappy with some of my work and I should leave. I suspect this referred to an estimate I did for some building work. I knew most of the builders were planning to have a strike. This would delay the job and make it more costly, so I built the cost into the estimate. This of course increased the price and made it uncompetitive. The sensible action would have been to accept we would not get the contract. Instead my estimate was binned and a more conventional estimate submitted. I heard later they had lost a lot of money on the contract. Sad, thought I.

I cannot recall the last time I saw a wagon displaying the livery of William Rainford, but there is still a company of that name in Cumbria. I suspect Rainford was another of those companies that could not survive the death of its founder. While at Rainford I had been offered jobs by a few local small companies. I accepted one of them and was employed as a bookkeeper. However, once I had been through the accounts it was extremely clear that the company was undercapitalised and had a large debt with a company in Sheffield that manufactured the product it sold. This was a flexible steel ladder that could be thrown out of an upstairs window to enable emergency evacuation. The only way the company could survive was to sell a large number of ladders quickly. The owner had dreams of advertising in the *Radio Times*, but I thought it unlikely they would offer such a small company credit. Without such advertising these ladders were unlikely to sell. It was clearly time to look elsewhere.

With the help of the DRO, I found a job as a credit controller at a newspaper. The principle of the job was simple enough. People advertised in the newspaper, but surprisingly few of them paid for their advertisements. As a consequence, the company had a poor cash flow and if it had not been for the support of the parent company it would have been in serious difficulties. My employer was West Cheshire Newspapers, which owned all of the titles on the Wirral Peninsula up to Ellesmere Port, where we faced competition from the Thompson Group. Most of our newspapers were produced weekly and included *the Birkenhead News, West Kirby News* and the *Ellesmere Port News.* The company was owned by the Liverpool Daily Post Echo, then under the firm control of Sir Alec Jeans, who was the third generation of his family to chair it. He also owned Stevenson's Newspapers, which had the monopoly of newspapers between Southport and Liverpool. As a consequence, if anybody wished to advertise in a newspaper between Southport and Ellesmere Port they could only do so in one of Sir Alec's newspapers, with few exceptions.

I was a member of the accounts department which was supervised by an accountant whose first name was Gordon but whose surname I cannot recall. Gordon was very supportive, although he was sometimes exasperated when I arrived late because of congestion in the Mersey Tunnel. My office was in Birkenhead and I had to drive from Liverpool, but most of the traffic was heading in the opposite direction. Of the four lanes in the tunnel, three were used each morning for traffic into Liverpool and one for traffic to Birkenhead. If a motor broke down it could lead to huge delays. His assistant was Roger, who was training to be an accountant and could always be called on for support.

The usual way the company sought to encourage people to pay was to stick a label on the advertiser's monthly statement asking if the "gravy train" was coming in yet. Predictably, these labels with their cheerful messages were ignored. I was conscious that my job was to get money flowing in. The largest amount of debt was owed by a relatively small number of companies, largely public relations firms and advertising agencies. These were known as trade advertisements, which distinguish them from the classified advertisements that were placed by members of the public or small companies. Instead of sending them silly labels I made a point of telephoning each of them several times a week, making clear we could not allow the balance to be unpaid. Some large cheques arrived as a result and I followed up these companies to ensure further accounts were paid on time. Some of the companies were strongly resistant to paying and saw delaying payment as a fair means of assisting their cash flow. But from the viewpoint of my company it restricted our cash flow and resulted in our seeking loans from the parent company. When I began to pressure them a bit harder for payment, the Sales

Director complained to Gordon and to me that I was in danger of discouraging people from advertising and needed to take a more considered approach.

It occurred to me instantly that any Sales Director could easily sell products or services if the buyer knew they would not be made to pay for them. To my mind this was not salesmanship at all. Given my history of drawing attention to the failings of my managers in previous companies, I said nothing. At a later meeting with Gordon I suggested that all three companies in the group should act in unison. If the large advertisers refused to settle their accounts we should refuse to take any advertising from them in any of the newspapers we controlled. This was bound to upset the sales directors in each of the companies, but I could really see no point in selling advertisements to companies that refused to pay for them.

Gordon played his hand well, and after a few weeks' delay the strategy was agreed by Sir Alec. With that support I could lean on the companies. The largest debts were owed by advertising agencies. If they could not advertise, their clients would move to a company that could. The result was that the cash flow position changed dramatically within a month. Instead of borrowing we were able to start repaying the loans from the parent company.

Although not as valuable in cash terms, classified advertising was an important source of income and contributed to sales. Most of these advertisements were death or marriage notices which were usually paid for promptly, although the invoicing system meant people received up to three months' credit before we began to seek payment. A significant proportion of classified adverts were placed as 'TC', or "'til cancelled". Unless these were managed the account would accumulate. Many traders used this system. Mostly they were window cleaners, electricians, aerial erectors etc. Instead of sending them pompous letters with threats implied, I would stay late two nights a week and call them at home. There was no use doing this during the day, as they would be out working. Mobile phones had not been invented. This approach enabled me to secure payment for most of these accounts, although in some cases I had to allow payment over many months. Most of these advertisers were not wealthy and lived on what they earned that week, and there was little point in pressing for money they did not have. My usual tactic would be to seek agreement that all current advertising would be paid for on a monthly basis. I would then agree payment terms regarding the balance, and providing these were met we allowed the advertising to continue.

On some occasions it was obvious we were not going to be paid and would need to write off the debt. On one occasion I telephoned an advertiser who had not paid for almost a year. His wife answered the phone and when I asked if I could speak to him she simply replied "No". I asked her whether her husband intended to pay the debt. She said, "I don't think so". I replied that I would cancel the advertisement immediately to prevent the debt increasing. I would then seek a court order for payment. She asked, "What does that mean?" I explained, "The court will require your husband to pay the debt he owes for his advertisement. If he fails to do so it moves from being a civil to a criminal matter and that could mean the court could impose a custodial sentence." "What's a custodial sentence?" she asked. I explained, "Your husband could go to prison". "I don't think he would care," she said. "He's in prison now and has been for months." A little research next day confirmed her statement.

There is no point leaving on the books of a company an asset that cannot be realised. In this and other similar cases there was little choice but to write off the debt. Despite the disappointing outcome to this case, speaking to these sole traders was often a pleasure, as they all had stories to tell and they had a wide range of life experiences.

My final task in the first year was to agree with Gordon and Roger that we should change the invoicing system. Invoices were issued monthly in arrears. At the end of a second month a statement was sent which gave the figures but which was otherwise bland. It was only after three months that we pressed gently for payment. I suggested that the first invoice should clearly state that payment was due within one week. When the statement went out a month later it would be clear that the debt was considered overdue. At that point I would telephone them. The result was highly favourable to our cash flow, and the number of bad debts, which had initially risen because it was clear some accounts could not be settled, was falling dramatically.

After a year Gordon called me into his office and said "Sir Alec has been looking at your work." I braced myself for defence. He then said, "He's been impressed and he's authorised a 25% increase in your salary." I was very conscious that without Gordon's help I could not have overcome the resistance of the sales directors. Apparently, even they were beginning to appreciate that sales that are paid for are more use to the company than those that are not.

Working for a newspaper provided other insights. The next office to the Accounts was where the reporters worked, and I had to pass through this office frequently. This gave me an opportunity to witness the heart of the business, where they generated or reported news to fill the pages of our various weekly newspapers. Because we did not publish every day, it was hard to have scoops, but our reporters had very clear ideas about what constituted news. School prize days and sports days were definitely news because with each picture of a different child collecting prizes we could be sure the family and friends would purchase about 10 copies. News was also generated by the various local authorities, but coverage was mostly polite as town councils were major advertisers. Some of the reporters had a particular skill for writing thousands of words on a topic that justified fewer than a hundred, but it all generated newsprint.

In July 1969 Prince Charles was inaugurated as Prince of Wales at Caernarvon Castle. As North Wales was not far away we treated this as a major local story. One of our journalists wrote a piece that was published over two pages in each edition in two consecutive weeks. It was entitled something like "My life with the Prince of Wales". I hadn't realised our reporters were so well connected, so I read the articles for the behind-the-scenes news. Virtually all of it was the usual biographical details that most the newspapers were using. As far as I could tell, the journalist's life with the Prince consisted of two rugby games that the Prince's school had played against the school of our reporter. I do not recall the results of the matches, but clearly my colleague's school had taught him how to spin out the story – an important skill in journalism.

One day we did have a scoop, and I played a small role in it. The window by my desk overlooked the old Birkenhead Market, which was mostly of wooden construction. While gazing out of the window I noticed what I thought were smoke fumes and said to the office in general, "I think the Market is on fire. What does anybody else think?" In the accounts department we all agreed that it was sufficiently suspicious for us to call the Fire Brigade. I picked up the telephone to dial 999 when a reporter, who happened to be in our office, said, "Don't ring them yet. If it does burn we will get some great pictures." At this point a photographer joined us and was leaning out the window to find the best shot. The Fire Brigade soon arrived, but the old building was quickly engulfed in flames and as it was late in the afternoon the *Liverpool Echo* had already gone to print. We were due to publish the *Birkenhead News* next day and therefore had the pictures of the burning market before our parent company. Later in life I would have a number of dealings with newspapers, TV and radio. The advice I received from our journalists in Birkenhead came in useful.

Chapter 6
Embryonic Activist

While I was spending my late teens job-hopping,
important developments were taking place in the wider
world. Some of these would collide with my life and
influence future actions and direction.

On 22 March 1965 a letter was published in *The
Guardian* written by Megan Du Boisson and Berit
Moore. It stated:

Dear Editor

*Common sense informed the whole of Mary Stott's
article (March 15) in which she outlined the existing
pockets of need and distress which the Welfare State*

appears to ignore; perhaps even to encourage by its insistence on the existing rules and regulations.

But we should like to talk about a particular aspect of her article: the need for provision of a disability pension for all who are disabled, the amount being in proportion to the degree of disablement. This need is more readily admitted in the case of an earning member of a family, but when the mother of the family, whose main care is the home, finds herself unable to run her home without a considerable amount of help, incurring great additional expense, then few people would support the idea of a pension for her, it seems.

And yet those who dissent would readily agree to the children being taken into care (at great cost to the community) while the disabled woman is taken into a "home" and the husband tries to live on his own, visiting the children and his wife. The cost of this in terms of suffering for all members of the family is incalculable and we admire with all our mind and heart the work of Ann Armstrong in this connection.

A recent article in your columns on "the chronic sick" was relevant to this, for sometimes almost a lifetime can be spent in institutions, and with the expenditure of thought and the money which would otherwise be given to hospitalising the invalid it would be possible to keep families together. We would suggest the foundation of a group, to which all societies, such as those with muscular dystrophy, multiple sclerosis, poliomyelitis, and other long term diseases would contribute their ideas and authority.

This group could be called the Disablement Income Group - or DIG. It would exist only to correlate the work of the other groups in regard solely to getting recognition for the right of disabled persons, irrespective of the reason for that disablement, to pensions from the State to enable them to live in a reasonable degree of independence and dignity in their own homes.

The principle of this idea is accepted and acted upon in other countries in Europe, such as Norway and Sweden; and possibly in others as well. At this point we declare our interest; we both have multiple sclerosis. But, taking up Mary Stott's challenge because "someone had to do it," we invite any person or society interested to write to us about DIG - the Disablement Income Group.

Yours faithfully
Megan Du Boisson, Berit Moore
Rellen House, Busbridge Lane, Godalming, Surrey."

The letter prompted a huge response and DIG was duly created, with Megan Du Boisson as its chair. Branches were set up around the country and it became one of the most effective campaigning groups of the 1960s and 1970s. Du Boisson and Moore's letter challenged many of the "givens" of the day. The first was that in supporting disabled people the government did not consider the extent of disablement or need but instead on how people had acquired their disability. There were pensions for ex-service personnel, and these were determined by the extent of impairment; points were awarded for the loss of a limb or sight etc. Industrial Injuries Payments were made to people who became disabled in the course of their work. Both of these groups were seen as worthy of support because they were contributing or had contributed to the economy and had paid into "the system".

People who had become disabled as children were excluded, because they had not worked. So too were people not in work who became disabled as adults, and this included many housewives. All these groups received was the normal means-tested social security available to unemployed people. Megan Du Boisson drew attention to the rather obvious fact that all disabled people incur extra expenses as a direct result of their disability. Not only did the government's social security system fail to acknowledge this, apart from in the case of veterans and people with industrial injuries, but also because disabled people faced these costs, those on the basic social security payment had to make that payment go further, and this had not been taken into account. As a consequence a disabled person was worse off than a non-disabled person receiving the same payment.

The demand was also reasonable. It sought no more than to get "recognition of the rights of disabled persons, irrespective of the reason for that disablement, to pensions from the State to enable them to live in a reasonable degree of independence and dignity in their own homes." Many of the disability benefits introduced in the 1970s were a direct result of campaigning by DIG. My first lobby of Parliament was in 1969 and it was arranged by DIG.

It has been suggested that DIG was the first pan-disability group in that it did not seek to cater for people with a particular impairment such as polio or multiple sclerosis. The letter encouraged all disabled people to join DIG. It wanted to work with other disability charities but was run by disabled people. Over a decade later the issue of who controlled disability charities would become a major topic of debate and argument.

Megan Du Boisson was killed in a road accident in 1969, but the seeds she had sown flourished. She had gently but firmly persuaded a growing number of Members of Parliament that disabled people needed additional financial support regardless of how they became disabled. Another remarkable disabled woman, Mary Greaves, who was a retired civil servant and an economist, succeeded her. It was the strength of DIG's research and analysis as well as formidable campaigning skills that resulted in improvements in disability benefits. One of them was the introduction of the Non-contributory Invalidity Pension, which broke the contributory principle. It gave extra money to unemployed disabled people regardless of their contribution history or the cause of their impairment. DIG no longer exists, but its contribution to improving the lives of disabled people was immense.

In 1964 the Labour candidate for the Wythenshawe constituency in Manchester was elected to Parliament and thus began the long and distinguished parliamentary career of Alf Morris. He came from a humble background. His father was disabled as a result of injuries sustained in the First World War. Morris saw how this affected the entire family and would often use the phrase "a disabled person means a disabled family". He was conscious of how little support disabled people received from local authority welfare departments, and how the inaccessibility of most buildings created additional problems. There had been no legislation to specifically support disabled people since that passed in the 1940s. Members of Parliament were indicating the need to do more about supporting disabled people but there was no attempt to introduce new laws.

Alf Morris was among the first to appreciate that the law needed to be changed. He travelled the country meeting disabled people and disability organisations.

I first met him in 1969 when he visited Liverpool, and it was impossible not to be impressed by his sincerity and humanity. He had a good understanding of how disabled people lived and realised that the social care provision for young disabled people often amounted to little more than placing them in a care home or a hospital. He was particularly distressed at the number of young disabled people placed in units with much older people but no one of their own age. He had raised this matter with the Secretary of State, Richard Crossman, who sympathised but took no action.[6]

Each year the House of Commons holds a Private Members' Ballot which all backbench MPs are entitled to enter. At this point the MPs do not need to say what their proposed Bill (ie draft Act) will cover. If people are drawn lower than seventh in the Ballot it is unlikely that they will be granted time in the busy schedule of the House of Commons to even discuss their proposed Bill. The top seven have greater opportunities, but few Private Member's Bills become law unless they receive government support. The government normally has a number of Bills it would like to become law, but the lack of Parliamentary time means they go onto the back burner. Governments have to prioritise and decide which Bills are most urgent. Time allocated to a Private Member's Bill is often used to promote a law that the

---

6. Kinrade D, Alf Morris - The People's Parliamentarian, National Information Forum, 2007.

government supports. In other cases MPs use a Bill to raise issues of concern but do not really expect it to become an Act of Parliament. Those who top the list have a genuine opportunity to present their Bill and for it to become law, although there are many obstacles to navigate.

In 1969 Alf Morris won the Private Members' Ballot. Any MP who wins the Ballot is inundated with draft Bills that various charities and pressure groups have previously drafted in the hope that an MP will support their cause. They will also be offered Government Bills that are guaranteed to become law and thus enable the MP to claim to have changed the law. This is an easy option, because the government will do most of the work.

Morris had these opportunities, but rejected them all. Instead, he decided to introduce the Chronically Sick and Disabled Persons Bill. In the following year it became the Chronically Sick and Disabled Persons Act 1970 (CSDPA) and required local authorities to compile a register of disabled people in their area, social services departments to provide welfare and social care to disabled people and public buildings to be accessible to disabled people as well as creating the Blue Badge Parking Scheme (then Orange Badge). This created enormous interest among disabled people and Alf Morris was inundated with letters and requests for help. He needed support in dealing with this and with drafting the Bill. Morris's battle to get his Bill through Parliament is detailed in his book "No Feet to Drag".[7]

In 1965 the drummer of the Salvation Army pop band the Joystrings spoke on the Today programme in the Thought for Today slot about the need for buildings to be accessible to wheelchair users. When not playing in the band, Wycliffe Noble was an architect who was advising the Leonard Cheshire Foundation on how to ensure their homes where accessible. Lady Hamilton, who, at the time, was chair of the Central Council for the Disabled (CCD) heard the broadcast. (The Central Council later became the Royal Association for Disability and Rehabilitation (RADAR) and subsequently Disability Rights UK.) Years later Noble informed me that Hamilton telephoned him, asked him to visit her and then suggested they should both travel to the USA, which was ahead of the UK in access provision. He later became a leading figure in drafting access standards.

Lady Hamilton, assisted by the CCD's Director, Duncan Guthrie, was taking it into political territory. She appointed a wheelchair user as Britain's first access officer. Within the CCD she created a Legal and Parliamentary Committee under the chairmanship of Mary Greaves and was thus well placed to provide administrative and secretarial support to Alf Morris and

7. Morris A, No Feet to Drag, Pan Macmillan 1972.

to deal with the sackloads of letters his Bill generated. The Council also supplied secretarial and research support to the newly-formed All Party Parliamentary Disability Group. This group of parliamentarians from both Houses was to become extremely effective and played a significant role in promoting the rights of disabled people.

While I was grumbling about the limitations of my Invacar, I was unaware that an organisation run by disabled people was already campaigning for the Invacar to be replaced by a Morris Minor or "Mini" car. It was the Disabled Drivers' Association, whose national management committee I was later to join.

In 1957 the National Association of Youth Clubs (now UK Youth) held a weekend conference that was attended by a disabled young man named Terry Rolf. He argued that he wanted opportunity, not pity, and in particular to take part in activities alongside his non-disabled friends. As a result the PHAB (Physically Handicapped & Able Bodied) was founded and through the 1960s PHAB clubs were established throughout the country. In 2017 it celebrated its 60th anniversary.

In 1968, what was then the Liverpool City Council Welfare Department, working with disability organisations, agreed to second a member of staff to be the Secretary/Organiser of a new organisation, the Liverpool Association for the Disabled, whose task would be to bring together the various disability groups in the city so that a unified voice could be presented to the City Council.

In the same year I was at work when I received a telephone call from my school friend Joe Woollam, who said "I went to a great club last night and you should come next week." "Go on", I said. He said, "It is called Fab and there are some cracking women there." I replied, "The last bit sounds promising but the name of the club sounds awful." Then Joe explained the meaning of PHAB, so I agreed to attend the following week.

It was an unusual setup. The club was held in two rooms of a residential home for disabled people. Disabled people outnumbered those without disabilities, but there was a sufficient number of the latter to make talk of integrated activities realistic. The person who appeared to be the life and soul and vaguely in charge was a large blonde middle-aged woman named Eileen Bleasdale. She gave a warm welcome to one and all. I discovered she was the newly-appointed Secretary/Organiser of the Liverpool Association for the Disabled (LAD), and that some of the non-disabled members had been recruited through Community Service Volunteers and were students at Liverpool University. Their dynamic enthusiasm soon brought in other non-disabled people, which was important as integration and inclusion were part of the goals of the club. I was surprised how important the club was for some of the disabled members until I realised that this one night was their only night out in the week. Young people wanted to meet other young people and have fun. Hardly an unreasonable ambition!

After I had attended for a few weeks Eileen Bleasdale asked me whether I would assume the leadership of the club. I agreed to do so and formed a small committee to assist me. A treasurer and the secretary were appointed together with a small number of other people who between them did the heavy lifting. Eileen gradually withdrew, but she was always supportive in the background.

PHAB evolved with a simple formula. We met at seven, had a speaker or entertainment at eight and broke for refreshments at nine. It closed at ten, when people normally reconvened in a local pub. The early meetings had been held in a residential home for disabled people located within Sefton Park, where our secretary Judy Bryant lived, but the council offered us better premises in a centre that until then was not used in the evenings. It was a larger venue with good car parking and plenty of local pubs. I remained as chairman until I moved to a college in Coventry in 1972.

As well as the Monday evening meetings, activities soon included weekends away, either with just our club or with PHAB clubs from other parts of the country.

We had very close links with Bradford PHAB. One consequence of all this mixing was that relationships flourished and thrived or died. A number of the members married people they met at PHAB and in that sense it mirrored the 18-30 Club on which it was loosely modelled.

The local authority gave us the premises free of charge, but we still needed to find funds to run the club, and these were raised by jumble sales and other means. We were eventually able to borrow minibuses to bring people to the club who had no transport. We soon developed a group of volunteer drivers.

From a personal point of view, the disabled members of PHAB gave me an insight into the difficulties they were experiencing. It was almost impossible to get their homes adapted to meet their needs. Others needed basic pieces of equipment that the Welfare Department should have provided. Unfortunately, people seldom knew how to navigate the system, and here I was able to help. I was also hearing of more and more cases of blatant discrimination where some of our blind members were refused entry into cafés and the like.

By this time I was using a wheelchair for part of the time as I was finding falling over increasingly inconvenient and painful. It was also at this time that I became conscious of the discrimination I experienced. Café and restaurant owners, even if their buildings were accessible, would stop me at the door and say, "we don't serve wheelchairs". I would sometimes reply "That's okay because I don't eat them." Even if I got my way, I was made to feel very uncomfortable. Using a wheelchair also restricted the number of places I could even approach as most of them had steps, which I could not negotiate. Using a wheelchair gave me much more independence, and it was safer than walking and less exhausting, but it meant that even a small step could prevent me making progress. It meant each day was a constant battle to move around the city.

If using a wheelchair resulted in facing discrimination, it was at least simple to get one. They were issued by the ALAC centres, which also issued Invacars. There were disputes over the quality of some of the wheelchairs being offered, but the principle that the NHS supplied wheelchairs to those who needed them was not disputed. During the Major Government it was agreed that disabled people could have a voucher to buy their own wheelchair if it cost more than an NHS one. This broke the principle that the NHS provided a suitable wheelchair to meet the user's needs. Later this was known as the Personal Health Budget, which suggests disabled people have control over their wheelchair budget. In fact it is the voucher with a new name.

Another area of discrimination was employment. If disabled people who did not use wheelchairs applied for a job they would receive a rejection on the grounds that "...unfortunately our premises are not suitable for disabled people". I was growing increasingly angry about the barriers placed in front of disabled people, but at the time I lacked the knowledge or experience to know how to fight it.

Eileen Bleasdale was gradually developing the Liverpool Association for the Disabled as an effective organisation in influencing local policy on disability. She involved me in a number of initiatives, which increased my experience. One day she told me that a meeting was being held to create a Merseyside branch of the Disabled Drivers' Association and suggested I attend. The speaker was the General Secretary of the DDA, Charles Pocock. He had restricted growth and was under four feet tall but was immaculately dressed in a hand-cut suit, had a clear and powerful voice and possessed a certain charm. Later in life I would get to know him well, but his speech that night was music to my ears.

He explained that the DDA had originally been known as the Invalid Tricycle Association and had been formed in 1948 by disabled people. It sought to promote the mobility of disabled people and was campaigning to have the Invacar replaced by a small saloon car such as those given to war pensioners. He argued for special parking provision for disabled drivers and thought there should be a national system to replace the current one whereby each local authority had their own rules and issued their own badges. He argued that this campaign could not be won from DDA headquarters but by involving disabled people from around the country. That was why he was hoping a local group could be formed on Merseyside.

I heartily supported the idea, and agreed to get involved. A chairman was appointed, and I joined the committee. Within a few months I was asked to represent the Merseyside Branch on the North West Group that met in Manchester. Within a year I was invited to represent the North West on the National Management. At the age of 19 I found myself on the committee of a national campaigning organisation, where I served for three years. I was young and inexperienced, but other people around the table were astute organisers and campaigners and I was able to learn a great deal from them. The chairman was Joe Hennessy; later in life Joe's path and mine would frequently merge and cross and I was able to draw on his advice and guidance for many decades later.

In seeking to replace the invalid tricycle with a car, the DDA had drawn on the arguments of social exclusion, the high incidence of breakdowns and the instability of the vehicle. These made no impact on the Department of Health because they did not regard the Invacar as a car but as a prosthesis, rather like an extension to a wheelchair. There was some logic to this, especially as the trike could trace its origins back to the early 1920s when the Red Cross put small engines onto Bath chairs. The two sides were talking different languages. The DDA subsequently promoted the argument that the trikes were intrinsically unsafe, and a number of high-profile celebrities endorsed this argument. One of them was the racing driver Graham Hill. As most of the trikes had fibreglass bodies, when they were involved in an accident the body fell apart and it made the accident seem much worse than it was. The resulting pictures made good copy for newspapers.

Later in life I was once again to face the problem of the narrow view that the Department of Health took of the world. In the 1980s Stephen Bradshaw was the chief executive of the Spinal Injuries Association, an organisation controlled by its disabled members. Bradshaw was always acutely conscious of the issues his members raised with him. One of them concerned hospital visits. An ambulance would call to take the person to their appointment. As they could not stand they would be transferred from their wheelchair into an ambulance carry chair, which comprised a metal frame covered by thin canvas. This could result in skin abrasions or even pressure sores which, in turn, might lead to a spell in hospital. Bradshaw's solution was to install lifts or ramps onto ambulances so that people could travel in their wheelchair.

I supported Bradshaw in a number of his meetings with the Department of Health where it was clear that they had no enthusiasm whatsoever for lifts on ambulances. Later, we changed tack and asked about the absenteeism rate of ambulance crews who had hurt their backs lifting patients. Apparently it was higher than anybody thought, and the stance of the Department changed. Disabled people getting pressure sores were not important, but staff injuries were. Now lifts or ramps on ambulances are standard, but initially they had nothing to do with the needs of the patient. It is Bradshaw's victory, but he achieved it by speaking Department of Health language rather than his own.

DIG had held two successful rallies in Trafalgar Square that were attended by disabled people from across the country. They had been addressed by prominent politicians and also by disabled celebrities such as Michael Flanders. I knew nothing of these until I saw the press coverage. However, DIG organised a lobby of Parliament in June 1969 and LAD arranged for a group of us to attend the lobby as well as providing transport there and back from Liverpool. The purpose was to press the government to provide disabled people with a social security income. It was not an aggressive lobby and MPs, including Ministers, responded positively.

It was on that occasion I met the future Prime

Minister Edward Heath in St Stephen's Yard at
the House of Commons. I asked him what the
Conservative Party policy was on disability benefits.
In my wheelchair I was much lower than him, and he
slowly looked down upon me, but before he could
reply a young woman with a notepad join us. "Who
are you?" he asked her. She replied, "I'm from DIG."
"Well, that is it, isn't it?" the great man replied. I never
did learn Heath's views, but I discovered later that he
played a significant part in ensuring that Alf Morris's Bill
received Royal Assent on the last day of Parliamentary
business before Parliament broke for the 1970 General
Election, which returned Heath as Prime Minister.

Through LAD and the people I was meeting
at PHAB, together with my role with the Disabled
Drivers' Association, I was becoming more active and
experienced in campaigning. In the late 60s I had also
found an evening class where I was able to the study
bookkeeping and commerce, with the result that I
acquired my first two GCE "O" levels.

In March 1969 my family left Tweed Street, which
was to be flattened as part of the slum clearance
programme. My parents had resisted incentives to
move out of the city to one of the new housing estates
and instead were offered a four-bedroomed house
in the Everton area of the city. For the first time I had
my own bedroom and we had an indoor toilet and

bathroom. No more hobbling down the backyard for a pee. The City Council appreciated that I would not wish to climb up and down the stairs too often and they therefore also fitted a ground floor lavatory in part of what had been a utility room. My sister Joan married in the same month, so she never joined us in the new home.

A year later, Eileen Bleasdale invited me to join the staff at LAD. The job title was something like bookkeeper/administrator, but as the amount of bookkeeping a tiny organisation can generate is rather limited it was clearly an opportunity to assist her in improving services and facilities for disabled people in Liverpool. In 1970 I therefore left the security of West Cheshire Newspapers to join this fledgling disability organisation.

1970 was significant for other reasons. Alf Morris's Chronically Sick and Disabled Persons Act had reached the statute book and would soon become law. It imposed a number of duties on local authorities. These included compiling a register of the number of disabled people in their area and providing a number of welfare services, including access to leisure and education facilities. It also required housing authorities to have regard to the needs of disabled people. An important provision was that requiring buildings to which the public were admitted to provide access for disabled people. The relevant section of the Act states:

Access to, and facilities at, premises open to the public

> *(1) Any person undertaking the provision of any building or premises to which the public are to be admitted, whether on payment or otherwise, shall, in the means of access both to and within the building or premises, and in the parking facilities and sanitary conveniences to be available (if any), make provision, in so far as it is in the circumstances both practicable and reasonable, for the needs of members of the public visiting the building or premises who are disabled."*

This was a major breakthrough, because it had the potential to ensure that buildings to which the public were admitted should be accessible. It did not apply to buildings owned by employers which were used only by their staff and not the public. Unfortunately, we were to discover just a year later that the phrase "insofar as it is in the circumstances both practical and reasonable" was to prove a critical weakness in the legislation. In 1971 we learned that Tesco had bought the site on which the Classic Cinema was located. They planned to build a small supermarket on the ground floor and relocate the cinema to the first floor. The Classic was one of the few cinemas accessible to disabled people in the Allerton area of the city and was used by them. Nearby there was a residential home for disabled people run by the Liverpool Spastics Society, which was not part of the national Spastics Society. At LAD we took the view that an accessible facility was being withdrawn and a lift should be fitted to provide access to the cinema.

Eileen contacted the office of the head of Tesco, Jack Cohen, and to our surprise he readily agreed to include a lift in the plans. We thought we were home and dry until the planning application was opposed by the Cinematic Exhibitors' Association (CEA), who were concerned that if the case was won, all cinemas would be required to be made accessible. This would be a large cost to their members. The Deputy Planning Officer for Liverpool Council was Theo Knucky, who, by coincidence was married to Eileen's sister. He was determined to press ahead, and the planning application was granted subject to a lift being installed. The CEA appealed but lost. They were however granted permission to appeal to a higher court, which they did, and the ruling was overturned. As a consequence the new Classic Cinema was built with no access for disabled people.

The CEA then presented the Spastics Society Home, Angus House, with a film projector so that the residents could watch films without going out. This gesture completely missed the point. Many years later I worked with the CEA on their policies relating to disabled people and they are now much more positive. But the case did provide me with a clear lesson on the difference between Parliament passing a law and its implementation.

None the less the CSDPA did give us plenty of work to do. Local access guides were produced to tell disabled people which buildings were accessible. The council was urged to create designated parking spaces for disabled motorists. They eventually created three, in a backstreet in the city centre. After a week they informed Bleasdale that they had not been used and they were considering removing them. They were persuaded not to, as most disabled motorists did not know the spaces existed. Now, although there are many more designated spaces, it is almost impossible to find one that is unoccupied.

One of the tasks with which LAD was charged was to investigate the needs of disabled people within Liverpool and to bring information of need to the attention of the appropriate authority. If possible LAD could also meet the need through voluntary effort. High rates of unemployment amongst disabled people remained a major concern. Eileen Bleasdale had heard of the work of Mary Greaves and of her report "Work and Disability" and invited her to Liverpool to see if she could suggest solutions. The outcome was "A Report on Work and Disability on Merseyside", published in 1973.[8] Her recommendations sought to improve the

8. Greaves, Mary, A Report on Work and Disability on Merseyside. Liverpool Association for the Disabled, 1973.

current system rather than radically change it, but the heart of the problem for many young disabled people was their lack of qualifications, which then limited their employment prospects.

On a personal level her visits enabled me to get to know a national campaigner whom I previously knew only by name and reputation. We got on well, and Mary Greaves was subsequently to play a major role in my career development. But from the first moment I met her she was encouraging me to obtain more qualifications. Easier said than done in 1970s Liverpool.

However, before her arrival I had some good fortune, thanks to Eileen Bleasdale's intervention. One day three nuns visited us in our office. Eileen instantly identified them as belonging to the Ursuline order. She said, "You're a teaching order, aren't you?" Upon confirmation she said, "Bert has been trying to find a night school to study "O" levels but they all have steps. Could you teach him?" They agreed to do so, and for the next year I received private tuition from these highly-qualified nuns, who were lecturers at a local teacher training college, now part of Liverpool Hope University. The nuns were wonderful but strict, and they expected me to have done any homework they recommended. This meant balancing it with a busy social life, which included many late nights.

My first lessons were on Tuesdays. I was still

running the PHAB club on Mondays and after the club I usually went on to a folk club on a ship, the clubship *Landfall*, which was located in one of the Liverpool docks. It was completely inaccessible and a friend, Roger, would carry me across the gangplank down a flight of steps into the bowels of the ship, find somewhere to place me, and then go and fetch the wheelchair. It was a bit of a palaver, but nobody took any notice. The folk club finished at midnight and became a discotheque. I seldom got home before 2.30 but still seemed to have the energy to follow the wishes of the nuns the next day.

LAD also took a more radical view than most on the subject of holidays for disabled people. The Liverpool Welfare Department had given a number of disabled people an annual holiday at what had been a miners' camp in North Wales. I presume this was vacant because the miners were by then holidaying in Majorca. One day Eileen Bleasdale received a telephone call from the London Borough of Hackney informing her that they were sending a group of disabled people on holiday to Rimini in Italy and were wondering whether a contingent from Liverpool would like to join them. She accepted instantly, and so it was that about 20 of us found ourselves in London, meeting the Hackney group and preparing to fly out.

In those days airlines had not developed complex procedures for assisting disabled passengers. Their main concern was whether the group included sufficient nondisabled people to help lift the disabled people on and off the aircraft. In these particular holidays "able-bodied help" was part of the package and we were self-sufficient. One difficulty concerned the number of wheelchairs. The airline was content to take the wheelchairs of full-time wheelchair users but not more. Therefore one of the LAD vehicles, with the word 'AMBULANCE' prominent on the front, because this produced a tax concession when buying the vehicle, was loaded with wheelchairs and some days before the flight it headed for Italy. The facilities were basic, but everybody managed. Eileen subsequently befriended a disabled travel agent in Liverpool and was soon offering a range of holiday choices to disabled people. I was later to spend much time seeking improved air travel for the disabled people.

There are many amusing stories of those early days, but I will restrict myself to one. In 1974 we were to holiday in Portugal flying into Oporto Airport. Arrangements had been made with the airport director to ensure there would be plenty of staff to help people off the aircraft. Then came the Portuguese Revolution. As revolutions go, it was relatively non-violent, but the workers exercised their newfound freedom by having a series of strikes. The Airport Director informed us that there would be one on the day of our arrival. However, we should not worry, as he would arrange something.

And so he did. After the other passengers had left, the plane seemed to fill with short Portuguese people dressed in white and with bright red crosses on their breasts. When they identified our group, four of them would grab a limb each and carry the person down the aisle, including on at least two occasions some of our people who were not disabled. Then from the back of the plane two people started singing from Napoleon XIV's 1966 one-hit wonder:

"And they're coming to take me away, haha
They're coming to take me away ho-ho hee-hee haha
To the funny farm
Where life is beautiful all the time
And I'll be happy to see those nice young men
In their clean white coats
And they're coming to take me away, haha."

Eventually we were all taken away, to our hotel!

Not all the holidays went well. When a group went to the former Yugoslavia, people from European countries filled the hotel. These people objected to having their breakfast in a room containing so many disabled people and the hotel insisted the group had breakfast in their rooms. When any of the Liverpool group entered the swimming pool the hotel staff would wait until they had left the water and immediately and very obviously pour disinfectant into it. Some of the group re-entered the pool on principle and the whole performance would be repeated. On the third day a more senior government official became involved and the group were made to move to another hotel, where I understand they were made very welcome. The incident does illustrate how even in the early 1970s some attitudes were still so dated, but similar slights would be familiar to most disabled people.

Another law enacted in 1970 was the Local Government and Social Services Act. Amongst other things, this brought together the various welfare-type departments in local authorities into the newly required Social Services Department. At the time it was controversial, because social workers supporting people with mental health problems rightly claimed they had no expertise relating to physical disability, children's services et cetera. It was argued that individual expertise would be lost. Whatever the merits or otherwise, Liverpool's small Welfare Department became part of the new grand Social Services Department. Contrary to expectations following the election of a Conservative government, significant resources were allocated to local authorities so that they could undertake their new duties.

One of these was to provide housebound disabled people with a telephone.

This was not as easy as it might sound. In those days, long before mobile phones, the only provider of telephones was the Post Office. It was normal for people to wait between six months and a year between ordering a telephone and having one fitted. The installation charge was expensive. A deal was reached with the Post Office Workers' Union whereby their members, in their own time, would fit the telephones free of charge and the local authority would then assume responsibility for the rental. This system worked well in its early years. A friend of mine worked for the Post Office and agreed to install two telephones a week. He later told me, "After I have fitted a phone I leave them a few days and then call to see if everything is working all right. I called one elderly lady who was delighted with the phone, but said she was worried about the cord. When I asked what the problem was she said it was a bit too long. I told her I could come and shorten it for her. But she said she did not want that as it would be too much trouble for me but "could you just pull in the cord from your end."

Another part of the CSDPA empowered councils and other public bodies to co-opt disabled people onto their various committees. I was still in regular contact with my former Youth Employment Officer, and she asked me whether I would sit as an observer on the appropriate subcommittee of Liverpool City Council's Education Committee, which I did for a year or so. I was at this time gaining a higher public profile through appearances in the local press and taking part in call-ins on the then new Radio Merseyside.

Overall, looking back, I think that despite many problems Liverpool City Council was bold and progressive in its policies to support disabled people.

In 1972 I had saved enough to consider changing my Invacar for a conventional car. A new one was clearly out of the question, but I knew that when their converted cars were about nine years old the Department of Health sold them at auction and a dealer in St Helens used to buy a few. So I went to see him. These cars still had the hand-operated controls fitted, which saved me £250 to buy new ones. The cars were Minis, and with a little practice I found I could get in and out and store the wheelchair behind the front seats.

However, there were two dilemmas. The first was to decide whether I could drive the car. The controls were different from those in the Invacar. For a start, there was a steering wheel. I had never used one before and did not know how much arm strength I would need, as these were the days before power-assisted steering was common. I was also unfamiliar with the controls. The accelerator was a lever located in the three o'clock position behind the steering wheel. This had to be pulled towards the wheel to accelerate. Just above this was the lever that operated the clutch. This was servo assisted, but it meant that when changing gear my right hand was using the clutch and the left was occupied with the gear stick. My left thumb was on the steering wheel, but there was no limb left to turn the wheel. To add to this masterpiece of design, a small pole that fitted into the floor to the left of the driver's seat operated the brake. This was detachable to aid transfer in and out of the car, so it was possible to drive off without the brake lever being fitted.

At the time the car was nine years old and needed repairs before it could be used on the road. Should I buy a car that I might be unable to drive, without testing it? There was no way for a disabled motorist to test drive a vehicle before buying it. Car dealers did not have cars with hand controls. None of the charities provided any facilities to solve this problem. I took a chance and asked a friend who was a mechanic to pick the car up for me, do the repairs and we would see what happened.

Happily, I found I could drive it, but then came the second dilemma. I could drive my Invacar on a provisional licence and because there was no passenger seat I did not need to be accompanied. I had passed my driving test in Mansfield, but this did not cover me to drive a Mini. To help buy the Mini I needed to claim the new Private Car Allowance and return my Invacar. Legally, I could not drive the car I had bought without a qualified driver accompanying me. This was clearly impractical, so the only choice was to ignore the law and apply for my driving test immediately and hope I passed. I did so, but I am not sure whether it was because of my excellent driving or because the examiner could see how important the licence was to me and was kind in his assessment.

Many disabled motorists faced these difficulties at the time. In the early 1980s the Department of Transport found an ingenious solution when it created the Mobility Roadshow, where disabled people were able to test-drive cars on a closed road circuit to see if they were suitable. But that was a decade later.

Changing my Invacar for a Mini also meant giving up the support services that the Department of Health had provided. If the car broke down, I was on my own. Well, not entirely. I joined the Automobile Association and soon discovered what remarkable engineers they employed. On dark nights on a rain-soaked Welsh hillside they would labour valiantly to ensure I could continue my journey.

During my time at LAD I spent a fair amount of time in North Wales. I was in a relationship with the secretary and spent many nights at her Liverpool flat, often with Al Stewart in the background. Her parents lived in Llandudno in a large house that looked like a seaside boarding house. Her father was a preacher, so when I was in Wales it was strictly separate bedrooms. Once in the morning her father entered my bedroom and said, "I've just been listening to a radio broadcast where they are asking for donations to help cripples.

I was going to send them one, but you're a cripple so I can cut out the middleman and give you the £5 instead." He then placed the £5 note at the bottom of the bed. His actions spoke volumes about attitudes at that time, even more so because he probably meant well.

One of my tasks at LAD was to prepare the editorial for the quarterly journal *Contact*, which was sent to all members to bring them up to date with whatever was happening. The name was intended to suggest two-way communication, and some members were in very close contact. Some years later when the Royal Association for Disability and Rehabilitation started, its director, George Wilson, telephoned me at LAD to ask whether they could use the title 'Contact' for the journal they were proposing. I checked with Eileen Bleasdale, who, of course, instantly agreed, and so it happened.

In the summer of 1972 I received the results from my "O" level examinations; I had passed all three. I now had the five O-levels I needed to apply to study A-levels. This was a big decision. I had been told throughout my life that I should not aspire to "O" levels, but now I had successfully done so the "A" levels were a possibility and nobody had told me they were impossible, probably because they were off the radar. I discussed the situation with Eileen Bleasdale and the nuns. Their view was that "A" levels were a realistic ambition and I should study for them. The difficulty, as ever, was that there was no accessible college in Liverpool. However, one had just opened in Coventry and I was granted a place. This meant resigning from my job, living on a student grant and taking the risk that it would be worth it. It was a huge risk, but I took it.

Bert in his pram on Roxburgh St., Liverpool,
c. 1950

Age 8, on the lawn of Greenbank School

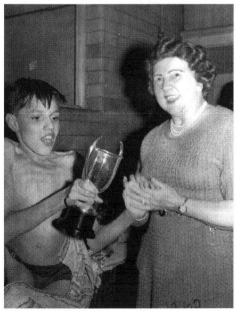

A trophy for early
swimming prowess, 1962

Enjoying scouting with a close friend, Arthur Brindle

Cub leader's wedding: Bert with lifelong close friends Scout
Leader Ron McManus, Joe Woollam and Gerry Kinsella

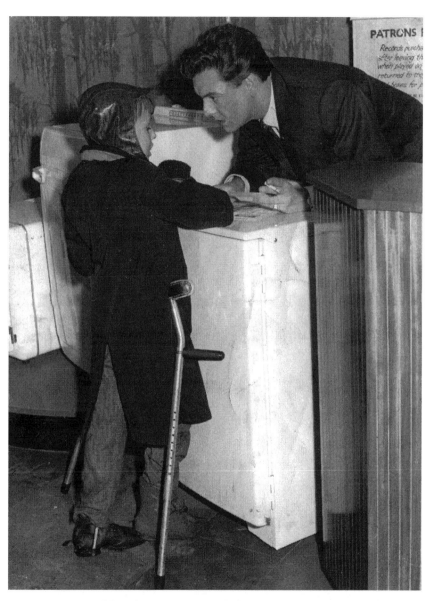

Meeting comedian Bob Monkhouse
(it was a friendly conversation!)

Flat warming in Liverpool in the 1970s, with brothers and sisters

The activist

Bert in his early RADAR years, c. 1980

With the then RADAR Chief Executive, George Wilson

Opening of RADAR offices in City Road, London with
HRH the Duchess of Gloucester and Sir Peter Baldwin
(then chair of RADAR), 1994

Testing bus
accessibility with
Transport Minister
Peter Bottomley MP

Testing taxi accessibility with leading racing
driver Sir Stirling Moss

With HRH the Duke of Edinburgh

With HRH the Princess Royal

With Prime Minister Margaret Thatcher,
promoting accessible transport

With close political ally Lord Jack Ashley

With Minister for the Disabled Margaret Hodge MP,
on DRC launch day 2000

With DRC Commissioners

DRC farewell party, 2007

Being knighted by HRH Prince Charles, 2007

Talking with HRH Prince Charles at the knighting ceremony

With Lady Maureen Massie and Bert's mother, outside
Buckingham Palace after the knighting ceremony

Post-knighting celebratory lunch with family and friends

Sir Bert attending and processing at Liverpool John Moores University during his long association with the University from his Honorary Fellowship in 2002 to subsequently serving as Governor until his death 15 years later."

With Prime Minister Tony Blair

The perils of intrepid holiday travel – near the
Great Wall of China, 2010

Celebration of Habinteg's 40th anniversary, 2013

Sir Bert Massie CBE DL

Chapter 7
The Semi-Detached Activist

Although I had expended considerable energy in obtaining my handful of GCE "O" levels, I had mixed feelings about going to Coventry. When I had moved to Mansfield five years earlier I had been working as a lift operator just to earn a wage until there was a vacancy at Portland College. I was not in a long-term relationship and was generally just enjoying life in a way that could be done equally agreeably in the remnants of Sherwood Forest. I was still leaving boyhood, and the roots of adolescence were still attached and dangling. The risks I was taking were not particularly great and the financial risk, which was more significant, was shouldered by the government.

Now I was in a relationship which was unlikely to survive my being absent most of the time, and indeed, it soon petered out. I was also taking a significant financial risk. Although my job was hardly well-paid, the salary was sufficient for my needs. It was also interesting, as I became increasingly involved in disability politics and the many battles to improve services for disabled people. In those days few people thought of the issues in terms of discrimination and human rights. This vocabulary would be adopted later. I had achieved some prominence on Merseyside and through the Disabled Drivers' Association (DDA), I had learnt something of the national scene. I had resigned from the Management Committee of the DDA because I could hardly represent the North West when living in the West Midlands.

Even if I did achieve the three GCE "A" levels, university was the next obvious step. Were any universities accessible? It did mean that it would be between two and five years before I could pick up on the aspect of my life that involved earning a wage. I was also anxious whether I had bitten off more than I could chew. In passing my last three "O" Levels I had received more support than any student could reasonably expect from their tutors. It was unlikely that Hereward College could match that degree of support.

Another emotion was a sense of irritation that once again I was expected to travel over 100 miles to gain access to education services that most of the population could enjoy within a few miles of their home. Was it really so impossible to build colleges so that they could be used by disabled people? Like many disabled people of my age at the time, we argued strongly against special schools because they were segregationist. Yet once again I was about to attend a college built specifically for disabled people.

On a different note, it was unlikely that disabled people in Coventry were receiving all the services to which they were entitled and there were likely to be disability organisations with which I could become involved. In my search to put behind me the poor education of my childhood I had prioritised "getting an education". It was now time to put my anxieties behind me and to get on with it.

Although Hereward was a new college it inevitably, like all institutions, arrived with a history. Local education authorities throughout the country were beginning to recognise that in the field of further education very few were able to meet the aspirations of the new Chronically Sick and Disabled Persons Act. Making new further education colleges fully accessible would be expensive and take many years. Coventry City Council agreed to build Hereward on the understanding that other local authorities would send disabled students to it. Although this was an expensive option if viewed on a per capita basis, it was a relatively economical way of making further education accessible.

There were a number of accommodation blocks arranged in squares. Each student had their own bedroom with washing facilities. Bathrooms and toilets were spread around blocks and were fully equipped for disabled people. Part of the ethos was to promote inclusion or integration, and Hereward was located immediately adjacent to Tile Hill College, which although designed for non-disabled people, included a number of features to enable people from Hereward to study there.

I was not qualified to judge how Hereward compared with conventional further education colleges, as I had never attended one. However, it seemed to me that they took themselves and their mission seriously. The staff at Hereward expected a high proportion of their students to go to university. For me, this was novel. Expectations were high.

In most further education colleges students tended to be in their late teens, but I noticed that at Hereward many of my fellow students were, like me, in their early twenties. The five years or so difference was the education gap that disabled people had to bridge. The missed schooling for medical or other reasons and the low expectations imposed upon us could be measured in years.

During the first years of Hereward's life it had

students who would later achieve prominence in a variety of fields. Nabil Shabin, an actor who later starred in the BBC drama series 'Doctor Who', was a student and a founding member of what became the Graeae Theatre Group for Deaf and disabled actors. Baroness Campbell of Surbiton DBE, then Jane Campbell, of whom more later, was also a student, and there are others I could list.

Hereward was successful in its initial task of helping disabled people through further education and into higher education. There was also a genuine attempt to treat students as adults, but inevitably it had its rulebook, which decreed that all students should be back on college premises by midnight. This was a bit inconvenient when spending evenings in Birmingham, and I often drove my old Mini through the side roads of the West Midlands until every rivet was complaining.

Hereward was clearly expecting to have students with high support needs, and each block had an ample supply of care staff who lived on the premises. This allowed the academic staff to concentrate on the teaching and getting people through their "A" levels.

The subjects I chose were sociology, English and economics. The lessons for the first were held at Tile Hill College. One of our first tasks was to sort out the supplementary courses. I noticed one entitled "Home Economics" and thought this was something to do with economic theory, so I put myself down for it. I was called in by the tutor and asked whether I had made a mistake. Clearly I had, but it proved fortunate. She had a vacancy on the typing course and thought this might be a useful skill for me to acquire, and as a result I became the only male on the course. Although I never achieved competence as a typist, I was soon able to type more quickly than to write and the resulting print was a great deal more legible than my handwriting. The lecturer was Jean, who I soon discovered was involved in a number of disability organisations in Coventry and Warwickshire as she sought to make Hereward part of the local disability scene. Through her I became involved in a number of organisations that operated on a local scale.

One organisation with wider aspirations was known as SPOD – Sexual and Personal Issues of the Disabled. This had been established by a group of people who viewed this as a serious academic subject in which people could be assisted by research. My task had been to help draft a questionnaire.

Communities featuring a disproportionately large number of disabled people contain, like all groups of people, sexual tensions, conflicts, desires and the never-ending search for opportunities to engage in sexual activity. Hereward was no exception. Given the age group, this was probably inevitable. There did however appear to be a relaxed approach to staff/student relationships and those between students. I knew many people at Hereward who were more than happy to talk about sex but mostly just wanted to engage in it. One friend, "L", was born with Cerebral Palsy. It left him with a slight speech impairment and one or two minor features on his face were asymmetrical. He was otherwise a handsome, well brought up and highly intelligent young man, so the fact that he did not have a regular girlfriend was always blamed on people's attitude to his cerebral palsy.

It was through his intervention that I first met the disabled activist and academic Vic Finkelstein. Finkelstein worked for the Open University on their disability studies courses and together with Paul Hunt had developed the social model of disability. L had contacted Finkelstein, who agreed to visit him at Hereward, and I joined for part of the meeting. Essentially, Finkelstein and Hunt proposed a new way of viewing disabled people and disability issues. Instead of seeing disabled people as the problem to be accommodated, they envisaged a world in which disability was normal and those who did not have disabilities as abnormal. As both Hunt and Finkelstein were wheelchair users, their early examples tended to involve such people. If everyone used a wheelchair it would be normal for every building to be ramped. The model also stressed that the medical profession generally failed when they tried to "cure" disabled people. Rather than invest our efforts into medicine we should accept that disabled people are disabled and build a society suitable for our needs. L was much taken by this argument. As a socialist he had long believed that it was the organisation of society that needed to change rather than moulding individuals to fit into the contours of a dysfunctional society. Many a night I had long discussions with L over this and similar issues.

One evening ended in much the same way as many of its predecessors, but before breakfast next morning I was informed that L was dead; he had hanged himself during the night. I'm not sure why I felt so guilty about this. I still have no idea why he did it. He would certainly have had a good university career had he taken his A-levels. Was it the lack of female companionship? Did he see Finkelstein's utopia as realistic or unrealistic? Or was he simply, as I have seen so many times, not prepared to climb the many obstacles society would place in his way before it would let him make the same progress as anyone else? No matter how many buildings and institutions appeared with the objective of "helping the disabled", most disabled people faced a hard struggle and like L, felt deeply alienated.

Outside the college the work of previous years was proving fruitful. In 1975, the incoming Conservative government of 1970 under Edward Heath introduced a non-contributory invalidity pension aimed at

220,000 men and single women of working age who had become sick or disabled before they had been able to accumulate sufficient contributions to claim sickness and invalidity benefits.[9] The NCIP broke the contributory principle that had applied since the creation of welfare state. Attendance Allowance was also introduced, followed by Mobility Allowance. The details are for another day, but during the early 70s the principle had been won that disability was expensive and that the State should make a contribution towards the costs. The way in which the changes to supplementary benefits for disabled people were made in the early 1970s would later have a huge impact on the evolution of those benefits, but the important point was that the government was now prepared to assist disabled people with the cost of being disabled.

In campaigning terms I had cut my teeth seeking to replace the Invacar with a conventional car. Sometime in the early 1970s I received a letter from a campaigner, Peter Large, whom I did not know at the time. He disagreed with my argument on the basis that to qualify for an Invacar it was necessary for a person to be able to drive the vehicle. If it was replaced with a saloon car, the additional complications would reduce the number of disabled drivers who would be able to make the change. It also meant that those who were

9. Irene Loach .Disabled Married Women. A Study of the Problems of Introducing the Non-Contributory Pension in November 1977. Disability Alliance 1977.

unable to drive at all would receive no help apart from the minimal private car allowance. He suggested it would be better for all disabled motorists, including passengers below retirement age, to be entitled to a mobility allowance and enabled to use this to purchase a vehicle.

The government was also beginning to address the issue seriously. A retired civil servant, Lady Evelyn Sharp DBE, was appointed by the Secretary of State, Sir Keith Joseph, in April 1972 to investigate the mobility of physically disabled people. Her report was relatively short, but it changed the policy landscape.

She started by making the point that if, as disability campaigners argued, the Invacar was inherently unsafe, the only responsible course of action for the government would be to withdraw them all. However, she rejected that argument and instead pointed out that the cost of providing an Invacar was now higher than for a conventional car. The issue then became whether providing cars would make the offer so attractive that many more disabled people would apply, so increasing the overall costs. She also recommended that disabled drivers and disabled passengers be treated alike. She recommended that the car should be provided through the NHS to people who met criteria such as needing a car to get a job.

For the disability lobby this looked as though the game was won, but when Lady Sharp reported in

1974 the political landscape was already changing.[10] Before her vision could take effect it would require the establishment of new financial arrangements between the government and voluntary organisations and the major banks. The outcome was the creation of the charity Motability in 1977, and although this eventually proved highly successful its early days were uncertain. It also demonstrated the importance of charities not overstating their case. Had Lady Sharp simply accepted the word of charities, she would have been perfectly justified in recommending the withdrawal of all invacars, thus leaving tens of thousands of disabled people immobile.

Finally, although Lady Sharp did discuss ramped pavements, she did not discuss public transport at all. It would be another decade before the newly-created Department of Transport would address this issue. Although I was monitoring such events and, to my surprise, I had been invited to submit articles to journals, I could not really describe myself as an activist. My main task at Hereward was to pass the A-levels. The tutors were invariably helpful and enthusiastic about their subjects. The English tutor extracted every ounce of politics from the texts he required us to read and the economics tutor would have found it impossible to hide his political allegiances. It all made for healthy and stimulating

---

10. Lady Sharp. Mobility of Disabled People. HMSO 1974

debate. Providing we did the work there was little reason we should not expect to pass the examinations.

Life within college was also more agreeable, as I develop a relationship with one of the support staff who lived in Manchester, where I spent many weekends.

During the end of the second term, the search was on for university places. Hereward were helpful in supporting students to get interviews, but the first questions at interview invariably seemed to be based around access issues and whether I would be able to manage at the particular university. My academic ability or lack of it was a secondary consideration. So once again I was being assessed on factors over which I had no control. Whether I could get up a flight of steps depended on whether there was also a ramp. Eventually, a number of universities seem to be considering my application seriously, but then circumstances in Liverpool took priority.

My parents' marriage was increasingly violent, and my mother spent a short time in a homeless hostel. This eventually resulted in her being offered a home on her own. I was unsure what I could do immediately, but I thought it would be better if I was at least in Liverpool. I therefore applied and was accepted by Liverpool Polytechnic and, as I was also homeless, I was offered a room in halls. The Polytechnic was then part of Liverpool City Council who, as ever, were supportive.

Sometime later I met the tutor, who showed me

around. My manual wheelchair just fitted into the lift, although both wheels scraped the edge of the doors. Had this manoeuvre been impossible it would have been equally impossible for me to enrol on the course of Social Studies as it was all held in the one building. I was also fortunate having my own car. At Hereward my 12-year-old Mini finally defeated the ageing mechanic in Kenilworth who had kept it roadworthy for me.

Just when I was running out of options, I received a letter from the wonderful nuns at Christ's College enclosing a cheque for £300, enough to keep me mobile with a replacement vehicle.

My first feelings about the Poly were of apprehension. This was the first time I had done any education in an integrated session, apart from the occasional classes at Tile Hill College. My anxieties were misplaced. I was with a terrific group of students, many of whom were my age. They were determined to involve me in the various activities, even where this meant getting my wheelchair into some of the most inaccessible pubs in Liverpool. Towards the end of the first year I managed to get a Housing Association flat in Liverpool which they converted to make accessible.

Life in any institution is made by the people it serves and all who work for it. I was fortunate in having an excellent team of lecturers, most of whom did far more for students than their contract required. I recall struggling with one essay when one of the lectures,

Mike Croft, invited me to his home that during the evening Mike took me through all aspects of the essay until I felt fully confident with it.

This support was also given by other students. On one occasion I left my briefcase on top of my car with a year's notes contained in it. Naturally, it disappeared. It did not take long for my fellow students to put a new set of notes together based on their own, and they were much superior to anything I had written.

I wanted to progress further in higher education, and was encouraged to do so. At Liverpool Polytechnic I took a degree in Business Studies and then went on to the then Manchester Polytechnic, securing a postgraduate degree in Social Work. My horizons were expanding, and my thinking was becoming more disciplined.

Chapter 8

Through the beam of RADAR

I was aware of RADAR some years before I was
employed by the organisation. In 1977, when I finished
my degree, the disability lobbyist Mary Greaves, whom
I had known for some years, invited me to lunch in her
book-lined flat in London. Amongst other things we
discussed my employment prospects.

She informed me that the Central Council for the
Disabled and the British Council for Rehabilitation
of the Disabled (BCRD) were planning to merge.
The merger had the full support of government,
which was likely to give it some financial support, at
least in its early years. I could see the logic for this

as both organisations were financially vulnerable. BCRD provided education and employment courses for disabled people and as appropriate would support projects. They were currently supporting the Association of Disabled Professionals, created by disabled professionals because none of the services provided by the government employment service were geared towards disabled people of professional or managerial status. I later served on the committee of the ADP but at the time was a member in my status as a student. Mary suggested I approach RADAR about a job the following year, as she knew I intended to do a further year at college obtaining a postgraduate qualification in social work.

She asked whether I had any plans for the summer break. Normally, I spent this working for the Liverpool Association for the Disabled as a way of gaining an income and also of keeping in touch with the changing world of disability organisations and politics. In the late 1960s she had written a booklet entitled "Work and Disability", and a number of disability organisations had invited her to update it. She was happy to do so but thought her own mobility impairments made it unrealistic for her to travel around the country. I could easily slot in this work between completing my degree and enrolling for my postgraduate course in Manchester. The updated report was published in 1979 and was entitled "Work and Disability 1977".

I had already indicated an interest in a number of posts in Liverpool but had received no positive feedback. The idea of working for RADAR was intriguing, but my initial plan was to do it for two years and then try again to find suitable employment in the North-West.

It had long been the ambition of the Minister of Disabled People, Alf Morris, to bring together all the major disability organisations to form one powerful one which could effectively represent disabled people. It had originally been suggested that the three organisations should be the Central Council for the Disabled (CCD), the Disabled Living Foundation (DLF) and the British Council for Rehabilitation of the Disabled (BCRD). In many ways they were obvious bedfellows. The Disabled Living Foundation had its origins within the CCD, where it had initiated many of its disability living projects and then developed the concept of rehabilitation equipment centres. Following some internal disagreement, Lady Hamilton set up the DLF as a separate charity and opened an equipment centre in Kensington, west London. The BCRD operated a number of projects supporting people with learning disabilities and also funded correspondence courses and, within Greater London, home tuition. Whatever the merits of these three disparate organisations, the DLF rejected joining forces with the other two, and although the BCRD did join the CCD I gained the impression that it was not an entirely happy marriage. It had been agreed that the title of the new organisation would be the British Association for Disability and Rehabilitation, but this received objections from Scotland as it did not cover that country. The Chairman of the CCD was the then Duke of Buccleuch and rumour has it that it was a brief word with a senior member of the Royal Family which helped result in the new organisation proudly bearing the word Royal. The records of the new organisation were meticulous, and when consulted recorded meticulous steps that were made to secure the Royal prefix. It is likely that a number of factors were at work.

Its director was George Wilson, whom I knew from his days at the CCD. Mary informed me that he would be looking for staff and suggested I apply. In the event, I did not need to do so because Mr Wilson telephoned me to invite me for an interview. As I still had a postgraduate course to complete, we agreed to consider a start date of autumn 1978. I was still hopeful that there might be suitable employment in Liverpool, but it was obvious that the Liverpool economy was moving in the wrong direction.

It was therefore in September of 1978 that I gave up my flat in Liverpool, left behind so many wonderful people, and with an enormous amount of help from the employment department moved to London. Initially, RADAR paid for a hotel room, which was not without its disadvantages as they did not seem to understand access issues! It was inaccessible, with a small flight of steps at the front. This meant negotiating with tourists to lift me up the steps. The bedroom was not much better. As soon as I sat on the bed it collapsed! I needed something more substantial. I had arranged with my landlord in Liverpool to meet another social landlord in London. This one specialised in housing accessible to disabled people. Within a few weeks I was offered a two-bedroomed flat near Broadwater Farm in North London. This estate acquired notoriety over a decade later, when a policeman was murdered during a riot. I found this part of North London perfectly agreeable and my neighbours did not appear anything like the people I later saw on television.

The fact that I was able to rent a two-bedroom flat designed for a wheelchair user owed itself to another set of remarkable circumstances. In the 1950s a group of parents of people with cerebral palsy had established the Spastic Society. It delivered a number of direct services, but soon discovered that housing was a major problem. Although local authorities were supposed to provide accessible housing, few did so. The Spastic Society therefore started its own housing association, Habinteg, designed to enable disabled people to live in the community. My flat was on Moira Close, named after Alex Moira, the then Chairman of the Spastic Society. The plan was to avoid building ghettos for disabled people, so one flat in four would be accessible. Mine was on the ground floor and had an inaccessible flat above it. This proved to be a great advantage to my Irish neighbours, who could visit and help me to consume my whiskey, though I was unable to visit them. But had their flat had the same accessibility standard as mine, it could only have been rented to a disabled person, thus helping to create a ghetto. The two adjacent flats on the ground floor provided partial access, but not to the same high degree as mine did.

On the estate Habinteg employed an assistant who could support disabled tenants. It was a perfect arrangement for me, as I could negotiate with my neighbours to clean my flat for me and to provide other assistance. Although I never intended to remain in London for many years, it was 2007 before I left and during that time I became a Trustee of Habinteg and was able to contribute to its policy development.

There were a few disadvantages. The first was that being London, parking was often a problem. Although Habinteg arranged a reserved parking bay for me, this was widely ignored by other tenants. Eventually we resolved the issue. Also, located close to me was a primary school and the caretaker had a two-storey dwelling close to me. He enjoyed a garden where he kept a cockerel that would sing a full repertoire of songs every morning from 5 am onwards. My attempts to persuade him to gag the cockerel, or even better execute it, were futile, and this difficulty only resolved itself when he fell ill and had to give up his job. Happily, his successor preferred to sleep in later than 5 am.

I often found it difficult explaining to friends in Liverpool why it would take so long to drive to work. The simple answer was the sheer pressure of traffic. Driving in London requires an entirely different technique from that in Liverpool. In Liverpool and northern cities, other drivers expect you to wait for a space and move into it. In London you are expected to create your own space. An average speed of no more than six miles an hour is common. It is surprising therefore that despite this low speed London has more speed bumps than any other city I know. When I was driving saloon cars, I could navigate the speed humps relatively easily, but once I began to drive vehicles converted to enable a wheelchair user to get in using a lift, other problems arose. Disabled motorists have two choices of lifts. One is fitted in the vehicle and invariably takes up some space. The other is to have the lift fitted underneath the vehicle in a cassette. This keeps the vehicle looking pristine but has the disadvantage that the lift cassette can easily catch the speed bump, and sometimes receive significant damage as a result. During my time in London I used both types of lift and eventually settled for one inside the vehicle, as I had a greater chance of getting home safely without damaging the lift. My lift was fitted to the side of the vehicle, which meant that if somebody parked alongside me, I could not deploy the lift and despite putting notices on the vehicle, this happened frequently.

The difficulty with London in the 1970s and 1980s was that most public transport was inaccessible and the only way of getting around the city was by car. However, on the positive side I now had a reasonably new car, a flat that was designed for my needs and a job. It was clearly time to start work.

Although RADAR was only a year old when I arrived, its formal structures were well established. When the Central Council for the Disabled (CCD) and the BCRD had merged, care had been taken to appoint an independent chairman of the Executive Committee. The committee minutes of the Central Council for the Disabled in 1976 also cast light on the financial situation of both organisations. Although they were both influential and carried weight within government and the disability community, both had very thin balance sheets and if the merger had not happened, it is likely that other solutions would have needed to be found to enable both or one of the organisations to continue. However, the merger was agreed and the structure of the two predecessor organisations had a clear impact on the structure of RADAR.

I had the grand title of Executive Assistant to the Director. In effect, the title was largely meaningless. I was in charge of 'Professional Services', the department that sought to give RADAR its cutting edge in campaigning and in ensuring disabled people could avoid segregation and enjoy inclusion. Each department had a policy officer and in most cases a secretary. The headings of the departments reflected the concerns of the day. These were access, education, holidays, fire and mobility. There was also an information service to ensure RADAR received the latest information, and we passed it on to members and people making enquiries as appropriate. Most of the posts were inherited, but my post was new, as was that of Head of Research and Information. From the British Council for Rehabilitation of the Disabled we inherited a Preparatory Training Bureau which offered home tuition or distance learning to disabled people. There was also a Disability Learning Centre in Regents Park.

It was recognised that there would be an international element to the new organisation, and this was the UK representative of Rehabilitation International, based in New York. A UK committee was formed to ensure liaison with RADAR's sister organisations in Wales, Northern Ireland and Scotland. The Association of Disabled Professionals had been part of BCRD, and although RADAR agreed to continue its funding it had no control over its policy. However, it was chaired by Peter Large, who was a member of RADAR's Executive Committee. Finally there was a section know as Remap, which consisted of panels of engineers from around the country. Many of these were retired and would accept referrals to design and make one-off pieces of equipment for specific disabled people, if that equipment was not available on the commercial market. Although this was a small service, it proved popular and still exists today as a separate organisation. It broke away from RADAR in the early 1990s.

The staff I inherited were at best varied. There was no master plan for creating a society accessible to disabled people. Indeed, the standards of what constituted access had not yet been drawn up. Within education the main debate was simply whether disabled people should be educated in conventional or special schools. In the field of employment there were no detailed figures on the employment rate of disabled people, and much of the debate was based around vocational training and whether the quota scheme should be enforced.

I was not really surprised by this, as the booklet I had written with Mary Greaves, "Work and Disability 1977", took a similar approach. The current system was examined and questioned, but an overall alternative was not offered.

Although RADAR claimed to be the coordinating body for disability organisations and was seen as such by government, together with an annual grant of £225,000 the claim was difficult to sustain. We had no expertise in learning disabilities apart from the very small unit in Regents Park. Nor did we have any expertise in mental health. Most of our expertise was concerned with people with physical impairments, and although we had organisations representing blind people as members we would look to them for professional expertise. There was therefore a question in the minds of some about RADAR's legitimacy. Equally, RADAR had nurtured links with Parliament and the civil service in a way many organisations had neglected, and during the 1990s a growing number of disability organisations sought to influence MPs.

Detailed work had been done on access provision because the architect Whitcliff Noble, working as a consultant to the Central Council for the Disabled, had put significant effort into ensuring that schools of architecture ensured their students knew something about access provision for disabled people. At the time no research existed on turning circles and ramp gradients, but there was widespread concern about disabled people being banned from cinemas or theatres. Such incidents were usually high profile and could be guaranteed to attract the media. It was all piecemeal. However, two events were to change that. The first was that in 1976 the UN General Assembly approved a resolution proclaiming 1981 as the International Year of Disabled People, with the UK as a co-sponsor. As there was no recognised national organisation representing disabled people it was agreed that the UK Committee should be hosted by the National Council for Voluntary Organisations, as it is now known. The majority of the committee were themselves disabled or the parents of disabled children (International Year of Disabled People, NCVO 1982. ISBN 0 7199 1079X). The Prince of Wales accepted the invitation to become Patron and the Earl of Snowdon, who was disabled, agreed to be president. George Wilson was one of the two Vice Chairmen, together with the disabled mountaineer Norman Croucher.

IYDP had a local feel to it. There was no huge central fundraising campaign, but local groups created their own initiatives. A number of national working groups were established and the heading of these gives some flavour of the approach taken. The groups were access, attitudes, leisure group, religious life, prevention, employment, family, information, residential care, housing, sport, technology, relationship group and the third world.

I was involved in a number of the initiatives. I was secretary of the Employment Group, and that led to a number of publications being produced by RADAR. I

was also involved in similarly larger initiatives, some
of which proved contentious, e.g. the Prime Minister,
Margaret Thatcher, hosted a reception at 10 Downing
Street. While many disabled people, including me,
attended this reception, there were already objections
by disabled people to cutbacks in provision for them,
and the reception was picketed by groups of disabled
people.

During the summer Buckingham Palace hosted a
garden party to mark the Year. RADAR was involved
in many of the detailed arrangements, and I recall
the huge difficulties we had getting so many disabled
people to London on the same day, given the shortage
of accessible spaces on the trains. It was a blustery
day, but it was the first time the pending Princess of
Wales was appearing at such a function. I noticed
that when she approached wheelchair users she got
onto her haunches so she could look people in the
eyes and speak to them face to face. This was the
first time I had witnessed one of the Royals doing this.
One disabled person asked her, "What will you do if it
is raining like this on your wedding?" she replied "Oh!
we'll just have to cancel it". In addition to the high-
profile events much was happening behind the scenes.
The UK government had been one of the co-sponsors
of the UN resolution, so it had to be seen to be playing
a full part. The outcome could not be measured in the
space of a year, but over a longer time-frame it can

be shown that preparations for IYDP led to significant improvements in provision for disabled people.

In June 1980 I was invited to a meeting at the Department of Transport. The meeting was set at a high level and was chaired by the head of the Department, the Permanent Secretary, Sir Peter Baldwin. He was accompanied by his Private Secretary, Ann Frye, who went on to ensure the Department transformed the mobility scene for disabled people. Most of the people attending were public officials, transport providers and disabled activists. This was an unusual mixture because it brought together for the first time people capable of devising public policy, disabled people who had a strong view on what was needed and the priorities, and the transport providers, who, at the end of the day, were the only people who could actually deliver accessible transport. At some point in the meeting I asked why London style taxis were inaccessible to wheelchair users. The taxi manufacturers, Car Bodies, pointed out that it would be easier to attach ramps to the wheelchairs. In response, I pointed out that there were just over 20,000 London-style taxis and over 800,000 wheelchair users. It might be more sensible to concentrate on making the taxis accessible.

I was to spend the next 20 years allocating a significant proportion of my time to the issue of making public transport accessible. The obvious objectives were to ensure that trains provided access for wheelchair users so that they could travel in a coach rather than in the guards van. And, of course how we could make buses accessible. The meeting discussed the various possibilities and priorities, concluding that the main priority should be making taxis accessible, because they provided door-to-door transport. To the credit of the Department of Transport they followed up with the taxi manufacturers, and during the 1980s a significant amount of work was done redesigning the black cab. I spent many days at their factory in Coventry looking at the various features on the mock-ups. The Department of Transport was admirable for including a wide range of disabled people which resulted in additional features being added. For example, the grab rails were tested by people with arthritis, who concluded the diameter was too small. As a result, we moved during the 1980s towards a taxi which was accessible for disabled people but also easier for everybody.

In 1989 I was invited to launch the new vehicle together with Sir Stirling Moss, but between the final prototypes and the finished products important inches had been lost from too many places and we knew the new taxi would not be acceptable. The manufacturers did not have the funds to redesign and rebuild and it was only through grants from the Department of Transport and the Greater London Council that the project was saved and eventually taxis were accessible.

In the early 80s I was asked to join an advisory group to the Minister for Transport, and in 1984 I suggested that this group should be put on a statutory basis. This was eventually agreed, and the Disabled Persons Transport Advisory Committee was created. Much of the progress in making public transport accessible can be traced to this committee and its working groups and to the dedicated team at the Department of Transport. This was just one example of how the International Year led to improvements in the lives of disabled people.

On a personal level, with the Employment Group, I co-authored documents on the day centres for disabled people, and with Melvyn Kettle of RADAR I published the first edition of the Employers' Guide to Disabilities. For some this proved contentious, because already it was being argued that people are not disabled as a result of a medical impairment but because of the organisation of society. The purpose of the publication was to guide employers towards informed advice on supporting employees with epilepsy or diabetes, et cetera. It was welcomed within Rehabilitation International circles and reprinted in a number of East European languages. However, some disability organisations in the UK dismissed it as being based on a medical model of disability, which in fairness was accurate.

Much of RADAR's work was concerned with analysing and recommending changes to legislation so it was more sensitive to the needs of disabled people. To do this successfully it was essential that the organisation was seen as credible, sensible and able to consider all points of view. Although RADAR had its critics, it also had close connections with a wide range of organisations both of and for disabled people throughout the country. It acted on a non-party political basis and would provide briefing notes to members of Parliament and Peers of the Realm. It also provided a research assistant to the Parliamentary All-Party Disability Group, which, in the mid-1980s, was chaired by Jack Ashley MP, a Labour MP, while its secretary was John Hannam, a Conservative MP. The cross-party nature of this group and its collaborative working were major factors in its success.

Although RADAR funded the research assistants and employed them, it was important that they followed the agenda of the APDG and were seen to be independent of RADAR. However, the connection gave RADAR access to a wide range of parliamentarians and also helped to keep it informed of issues which a wide range of disability organisations considered important. This was questioned towards the end of 1986 when the *Sunday Times* (23 November 1986) ran an article headed "Charity boss faces call to leave the job." The essence of the article was that the Charity Commission had decided to conduct an investigation into RADAR after allegations of poor management and in particular the way George Wilson treated staff. A number of the allegations were made by a former employee of one of the organisations that had merged to form RADAR in 1977. Knowing something of the inside of the organisation and of the allegations made by the *Sunday Times* they seemed insignificant; although there were staffing issues, they were not serious. The *Sunday Times* was deeply concerned that RADAR had an account with a wine merchant. I do not doubt this was true because everything purchased needed to be accounted for and it was far more efficient and provided an effective audit trail if this was done through formal accounts rather than through petty cash or via people's personal expenses. One outcome was a staff restructuring which included a slight change in my role.

Although I thought the article had little substance, it was taken seriously and consideration was given to suing the *Sunday Times* over the inaccuracies, but such litigation is never risk-free and after much discussion on whether it was an effective use of charitable funds it was decided not to do so. However, all the relevant players were contacted, as a result of which there was no formal Charity Commission investigation, MPs and others rallied round and relationships with Government were maintained. We received no negative feedback from disability organisations who knew RADAR well.

Nonetheless, such an attack leaves its mark.
Charities are always in a vulnerable position, because
different groups have different expectations of
them. Using charitable funds to defend the charity
or individuals is always open to criticism, although
Government departments use taxpayers' money in
much the same way without criticism. Next week
there will be another story about another organisation
and the press machine moves on. But I witnessed
the scars it left behind. When other people forget,
the principal characters still feel the pain of those
scars. My own view is that the attack on Wilson was
unjustified. He managed staff as though he was a
head teacher, and there were plenty of ways to get
around that.

The other major event was the publication of the
Report of the Committee on Restrictions Against
Disabled People (CORAD). This report was launched
in 1982 and defined discrimination on the grounds of
disability broadly. Its solution was that there should be
legislation to make discrimination on the grounds of
disability illegal and that there should be a regulatory
body or Commission with powers to investigate,
conciliate and if necessary take legal action on
individual complaints of discrimination. It should also
recommend guidelines on the reasonable affirmative
action required to accommodate disabled people and
to promote the integration of disabled people into

society. It made a total of 42 recommendations, but the early ones set the scene for a different way of viewing discrimination and acting against it.

At the time CORAD did not talk about civil or human rights but as in previous disability-related campaigns it focused on enabling disabled people to participate fully in society. To this end it stated: "the law should cover all areas where discrimination occurs, and particularly employment, education, the provision of goods, facilities and services, insurance, transport, property rights, occupational pension schemes, membership of associations and clubs and civic duties and functions".

Some of these provisions had already been made in relation to gender and race. A major change in the disability proposals was borrowed from the United States of America, where it was suggested that it might be necessary to take reasonable affirmative action to ensure disabled people could enjoy access to goods and services. This moved the argument from simply an obligation not to discriminate to a duty to look at what action could be taken to avoid inadvertent discrimination. CORAD did not get involved in philosophy but concentrated on practical measures. For example, it recommended that an Access Committee for England should be established to help draw up guidelines on access and to support local access groups. It was duly established and Peter Large and I became members of it. One of the

outcomes of this initiative was the introduction of
Approved Document M of building regulations, which
specified the precise access provision that should be
made for disabled people and which could be enforced
through the application of building regulations.
Inevitably, this did not prove entirely satisfactory, but
it was the first major breakthrough in enabling local
authorities to enforce an access code. The Building
Regulations were themselves a result of CORAD.

When the Report was published one of the first
responses came from the chairman of the All-Party
Disablement Group, Jack Ashley MP. He published a
Private Member's Bill to outlaw discrimination against
disabled people. As explained in a previous chapter,
it is extremely difficult for an MP to succeed in having
a Private Member's Bill accepted, but it does gain
publicity for the issue. In the early 1980s the Thatcher
Government had no compulsion in dismissing the
need for anti-discrimination. They argued that it would
be too expensive to implement, and in any event the
majority of discrimination was not malicious but took
place because people did not understand the needs
of disabled people. The answer was to educate and
persuade. As cases of discrimination were analysed
more deeply this argument became increasingly
untenable. However, there was huge resistance to
the concept of legislation. Restaurateurs argued that
they could not possibly make all their restaurants

accessible. Others argued that legislation cannot make people love each other, which seemed to be what disabled people wanted. Peter Large's response to this was he did not care whether people loved him. What he cared about was how people behaved towards him and legislation could regulate people's behaviour. CORAD had set the tone.

It certainly influenced the work of RADAR. In our campaigning and lobbying work we had two main approaches. When the government introduced legislation on whatever issue, we would ask if the legislation would have an adverse impact on disabled people. If so, we would make the appropriate representations with a view to resisting it. Alternatively, was there an area of human activity in which disabled people were being disproportionately adversely affected and, if so, what was the best way of resolving it? There were a number of options, one of which would include encouraging the government to legislate. Given the pressure on parliamentary time that any government faces this is always a long-term strategy, as legislation is never passed quickly. In taking a view of legislation, RADAR and other disability organisations would assess its particular impact on disabled people compared to non-disabled people.

One example was the introduction of the Community Charge, or poll tax, in 1990. This provided for a single flat rate per capita tax on every adult at a rate set by their local authority. It replaced the long-established council rates and in so doing removed a number of concessions disabled people had won over the years. For example, wheelchair users received a discount because it was recognised they needed extra space. The Community Charge was highly political and we were unsuccessful in having it amended. It was sufficiently contentious that it is thought to be one of the policies which led to the removal of Margaret Thatcher as Prime Minister.

In 1993 it was replaced by Council Tax, which was related to the size and value of the property. Peter Large and I saw an opportunity to regain the losses of previous years and proposed to the new minister, Michael Portillo, that wheelchairs users should have a reduction and their homes should be valued at a band lower than it would normally be. We also suggested a reduction for those who needed a garage and a minor reduction for those disabled people paying band "A" of the Council Tax, which was the lowest band. To our surprise, Portillo instantly agreed the major amendment, to allow the homes of wheelchair users and premises that had been adapted to be placed into a lower tax band. He not unreasonably rejected the idea that people on the lowest band could be paying more and whereas the Department of Health had made a big issue of garages in the 1950s for people who needed an Invacar, Portillo saw no such link.

Nonetheless, it was relatively small initiatives and interventions such as this that improved conditions for disabled people.

Each year a backbench Bill was introduced on anti-discrimination legislation, but it was not until 1994 that an opportunity came when the weakened government was facing increasing difficulty in resisting legislation. The Disability Discrimination Act 1995 was the consequence, but before then a number of small and incremental changes were made to regulations or incorporated into other laws. Although it seemed like a lost 14 years, progress was being made, if on a piecemeal basis. Nonetheless, I recall working with colleagues on rewriting the fire regulations so that they were more sensitive to the needs of disabled people, the Department of Health established a working party looking at access to hospitals and a new code was produced. The transport providers made enormous progress working with disabled people on how to make public transport accessible.

When we looked at accessible buses, we considered whether to have high floor buses fitted with lifts, such as those in the United States, or look at low floor buses which provided better access to everybody. The better option was agreed to be lowered floors, so that everybody could avoid the steps and get on and off more easily. Having looked at examples in Germany and Holland, opinion moved towards this.

The Department of Transport was concerned about one issue. If the wheelchair had to be clamped in to avoid it tipping over, this would mean the driver having to vacate the driving seat, with the subsequent risk that any cash takings might be stolen. It was decided to run a trial to test whether a wheelchair user could be tipped out of their wheelchair during normal traffic conditions. A low-floor vehicle was borrowed and taken to the government Test Laboratories in Crowthorne and I was invited to volunteer as the dispensable disabled person to see whether the driver could tip me out of the wheelchair. The driver chosen was Andrew Braddock of London Transport.

Braddock turned the bus on two wheels, and although the wheelchair moved and rocked around, it never fell over. This meant that if we used low-floor buses there was no reason why the bus companies should object.

While this detailed work was taking place quietly behind the scenes, there was a growing campaign for anti-discrimination legislation. Each time the government resisted a Private Member's Bill it simply built up more force for the next attempt. The government attempted to ease this pressure by giving away incremental changes which meant the agenda, which had seemed very lengthy, was slowly being delivered.

Unfortunately, disability organisations were not united in their approach. In 1981 the British Council of

Organisations of Disabled People was formed and only organisations which were controlled by disabled people were permitted to be members. It was argued that only such organisations had the legitimacy to speak on behalf of disabled people. RADAR and organisations such as MENCAP, SCOPE, RNIB etc. were seen as controlled by non-disabled people and therefore not entitled to speak or act on behalf of disabled people. This invariably led to disputes in the press and in other public forums. As the various organisations sought to obtain legitimacy and work together, an organisation had been established called Voluntary Organisations in Favour of Anti-Discrimination Legislation against Disabled People. RADAR's position was not assisted by its support for Bills that were not as comprehensive as some would like, but arguably had a greater chance of being accepted. RADAR's Executive Committee accepted the need for legislation but was neutral on whether it could all be introduced in one Bill. This gave the impression that they were less than enthusiastic about the legislation. In the mid-80s RADAR clarified its position and received a number of letters from disability organisations congratulating it on doing so. Even the impression that RADAR was not fully in support of such legislation was damaging to the organisation, and, of course, to the ultimate goal of many disabled people.

In 1990 I became the Director, or Chief Executive, of RADAR, and in that capacity I needed to employ a new Research Officer to the All-Party Group. I liaised with the chairman and the secretary of the Group, Jack Ashley and John Hannam respectively. I noticed that one candidate, Victoria Scott, had indicated that her father was a member of the government. This clearly needed checking, and it emerged that she was the daughter of the Minister for Disabled People, Nicholas Scott. This was an unusual situation. Did it disqualify her? It was clear from Victoria's CV that although her father was a Conservative her political views leaned to the left, but in any event the post required the successful applicant always to act with political neutrality as they were serving the entire group, regardless of political allegiance. It was inevitable that people in such posts held political opinions. Virtually all my staff did. The important issue was that the organisation was politically neutral. It needed to be managed rather than squashed or ignored.

Both Ashley and Hannam were content for Victoria to have the job if she was the strongest candidate following the interview. Even in a strong field of candidates she was clearly the strongest and was therefore appointed. Victoria Scott thus became RADAR's Parliamentary Officer and Research Assistant to the Parliamentary All-Party Disability Group.

Since the start of the campaign for legislation in the UK, the US Government had passed the American with Disabilities Act 1990, and this contained a number of provisions which we would wish to include in UK legislation. Victoria Scott received an offer from a commercial company offering to fund her to spend a few weeks in the USA looking at the American legislation. This had some attractions, as we needed more information, but it did not take long for Victoria to realise that the company had also picked up on the fact she was her father's daughter and this was influencing their decision. Her integrity left no choice but to turn down the offer. I therefore suggested to her that she should apply for a Churchill Scholarship, which would enable her to do much the same thing. Her application proved successful and she wrote a useful report. In 1994 she was interviewed on the Radio 4 Today programme, which revealed the identity of her father. Suddenly this became the press story of the week. Not only was Victoria principled and highly intelligent, she also had a winning personality and photogenic looks. To this extent she was a gift for the media.

While this story was filling the media I had been on a one-day visit to France to visit the manufacturers of the Airbus with a view to them installing a lavatory that disabled people could use. They had designed one which was essentially two lavatories alongside each other but allowed easy removal of the middle screen, thus doubling the size of the toilet. One of the problems people who cannot stand face is pulling underwear up and down, unless they have sufficient room to rock on their buttocks so the underwear can be raised or lowered as appropriate. The design was ingenious, but unfortunately it is the airlines who specify the design of the lavatories on aeroplanes and not the manufacturer, so this ingenious idea never saw light of day.

I had flown back into Bristol at about 7 pm to be phoned by Moyra Carey, one of my colleagues, about what had been happening all day. I immediately called Victoria Scott to ask how she was and whether she would like me to go round to her home immediately I got to London. She was, predictably, completely calm and collected and said the situation was now under control, the journalists had left and we could discuss it tomorrow morning in the office. It was the calibre of staff at RADAR that they could deal with any incidences like this, whereas in many large companies and public authorities a whole team of public relations people would be involved.

Despite the massive media attention Victoria received, I can recall only one time when she grew angry with a newspaper. As I arrived at the office one morning, she was fuming at one paper. "Look what they are claiming now!" she demanded. I read the piece and it did not seem malicious. "And the offensive bit is?" "Look," she said, "they are claiming I wear Doc Martens. I don't think I have ever worn them in my life!"

Chapter 9
The Disability Rights Commission Lives!

In the autumn of 1999 a letter arrived in my letterbox from the Secretary of State for Employment, inviting me to be the first Chair of the Disability Rights Commission (DRC). I was thrilled and honoured. It was the culmination of my career, as well as a huge challenge on behalf of disabled people. I replied in the affirmative by return of post.

When the Disability Discrimination Act (DDA) received Royal Assent in 1995 the then Conservative Government did not make provision for an accompanying Commission as had been established following the Race Relations and Sex

Discrimination Acts in the mid-1970s. There had
been explicit objections from political heavyweights
in the Conservative Cabinet. But I feared, as did
many others, that in the absence of an equivalent
to the Commission for Race Equality and the Equal
Opportunities Commission, the DDA would be largely
ineffective or, in the later phrase of Lord Jack Ashley,
like a car without an engine. The lack of a Commission
was in itself a form of discrimination against disabled
people.

Its absence led to intense lobbying by the disability
movement, aimed in particular at the resurgent Labour
Party and leading to a commitment in the Labour
Manifesto for the 1997 General Election to enact a
Disability Rights Commission. Tony Blair led the Party
to a sizeable victory and the new Administration's
first step towards the Commission was to establish
the Disability Rights Task Force (DRTF), with two
main purposes: to map out the roles and functions of
the future independent DRC (the subject of the Task
Force's interim report in April 1998) and to recommend
means of strengthening the content and impact of the
DDA.

That second report[11] ranged widely and made
a large number of recommendations, including
ones on education, the role of the public sector,

11. "From Exclusion to Inclusion", A Report of the Disability
Rights Task Force on Civil Rights for Disabled People
December 1999

the participation of disabled people in public life, employment, transport, the definition of disability and the scope of the DDA. The DRTF was ably chaired by Margaret Hodge MP, Parliamentary Under Secretary at the then Department for Employment (later Education and Employment, DfEE) and comprised 24 members drawn from the range of disability organisations (including myself as RADAR Chief Executive), employer bodies and other experts.

The DRTF proved valuable and influential. It provided a forum for in-depth discussion and informed agreement on the issues, involving the spectrum of interested parties. It covered a large amount of ground, in a professional manner and on time. It was also well served by its secretariat of civil servants (most of whom had been involved in the passage of the DDA and would later form the Departmental sponsor team for the DRC). A significant number of the DRTF members went on, through competition, to become commissioners (board members) at the DRC or important partners for the DRC's work.

The Task Force's recommendations had an important bearing on disability rights legislation in the following years and also contributed significantly to the Commission's policy agenda. It was in my view a good example of how the ground should be prepared for legislation, policy and establishment of major public bodies. Most relevantly to this chapter, its initial

report on the prospective DRC was accepted by the
government, which then published a White Paper
with plans to establish the Commission. The Disability
Rights Commission Bill was brought before Parliament
in 1999. It had a largely uncontested passage
(Theresa May proved constructive in the lead for the
Conservative Opposition) and received Royal Assent
in July that year.

The process for selecting the DRC Chair then
began in earnest, under the strict procedures and
criteria required of all public appointments. Following
my application I was shortlisted for interview by the
appointments panel together with, I later learned,
five other candidates (although I was never told
their names). The panel's assessments and
recommendation were submitted to the Secretary
of State (David Blunkett). I had met David on a few
previous occasions, but I do not think this swayed his
decision to appoint me. I feel confident that he would
also have met at least a number of the other shortlisted
candidates, and that the key factors for him were my
track record on disability issues and the range of my
contacts. Certainly they were among the main factors I
advanced to support my application. I have also been
asked whether my being a member of the Labour
Party might have played a part. I doubt that it would
have been a major consideration, but it is true that, in
addition to a candidate's direct suitability for a post, it

helps if he or she is broadly on the same wavelength as the government of the time. That is likely to help the conduct of business with Ministers, and so it proved in the case of the DRC.

Immediately following my appointment, I was involved in two main tasks, the selection of the DRC commissioners and of the Chief Executive. Under the DRC Act, both sets of appointments were to be made by the Secretary of State. But it clearly also made absolute sense for the Chair to be part of the interview and selection panels, together with an independent expert and a senior departmental official, and to contribute in a major way to the decisions. The outcomes would have a huge bearing on the expertise and strength of leadership within the Commission and on the quality of support available to me in fulfilling my role and responsibilities as Chair.

In legal terms, the Commission consisted of the commissioners. The Act provided for the appointment of up to 15 commissioners (including the Chair), who collectively bore responsibility for the effectiveness of the DRC in fulfilling its statutory duties. In addition the importance of the Commission lay in ensuring high-quality strategies and plans, the right and timely policies on major issues, determining priorities and holding managers and staff to account for delivery and for efficiency. Commissioners would play an important ambassadorial role for the DRC and be a source of insight and intelligence on the environment in which the Commission would operate. Individual commissioners would also as appropriate join working parties on the preparation of Codes of Practice, or the teams taking forward formal investigations and other inquiries, or the action groups subsequently established on learning disabilities, mental health and neurodiversity. It was therefore vital to choose the right people.

In particular I wanted a Commission that was determined to secure and promote the rights of disabled people, but which as far as possible also contained people from the key groups and interests whom the DRC was to serve and needed to work with. These included disabled people of course, across a wide range of disabilities, visible and non-visible; employers and providers of services (crucial to effective implementation of the law and good practice); and legal experts. They were drawn too from the private, public and voluntary sectors as well as the trades union movement and ethnic minorities. In practice there was no shortage of quality candidates, again selected under the Civil Service's rules and processes.

I was fortunate to have able and committed commissioners throughout the DRC's life. Typically two-thirds of them were disabled (including, I understand, the first person with significant learning disabilities to sit on a major public board). But I was also keen that the Commission included non-disabled people. DRC needed to attract the best talent and expertise. The main focus of its work was in effect by various means to change the practices and mind sets of the non-disabled world, and we needed to understand – and to show that we understood – the factors at work in that world if we were to move things on.

There was considerable stability in the membership of the Commission over the seven-year life of the DRC. Inevitably there were some changes to reflect the Commission's evolving priorities and the competing demands on some commissioners' time, and two of the disabled commissioners suffered untimely deaths connected with their conditions. But it proved possible to sustain the quality of the Commission throughout. It would be unfair and perhaps invidious for me to single out particular commissioners. Their overall abilities and commitment were demonstrated by the senior and influential positions they held or had held outside the DRC or went on to hold (three, for example, subsequently became Peers in the House of Lords and others received honours).

But I should add that I was especially fortunate in my choice of Vice Chairman, John Hougham. John, who is non-disabled, had previously, among other roles, been Director of Human Resources at the Ford Motor Company UK and then Chair of the Advisory,

Conciliation and Arbitration Service (ACAS). I do not think I could have been better supported or advised, and I personally and the Commission benefitted hugely from John's great experience, good sense and wisdom.

The second initial major task was selecting the DRC's Chief Executive (CE), with a further open competition under the same rules and procedures as for the Chair and commissioner positions. I was again part of the panel. The process was not completed until November 1999, when Bob Niven was appointed. Bob was the senior civil servant at the Employment Department and for several years had responsibility for policy and legislation on gender equality (including oversight of the Equal Opportunities Commission), race relations at work and in education, and disability rights. Because of the latter, once he put in his application, he absented himself from any issue touching on the DRC.

Among his previous posts Bob had been (the then) Mrs Thatcher's day-to-day representative on earth – well, in Brussels and London – on one of her least favourite issues (EU employment and social legislation), and was later a senior member of the Cabinet Secretariat during John Major's time as Prime Minister. At first sight it might have appeared that Bob and I were rather different kettles of fish given my background, education and disability activism. In contrast, Bob was non-disabled, had a comfortable middle-class upbringing, went to public school and Oxford, and had been a career civil servant. But we had met previously (including at DRTF meetings), and when we talked in private before the appointment was confirmed, we decided we were compatible. In practice it proved to be a first-class working relationship. Bob resigned from the Civil Service and took up the CE post at the beginning of December 1999. He did an excellent job throughout the Commission's eight-year life and played a key part in the DRC's success, thoroughly deserving his CBE in 2006.

At the end of 1999 I first stepped into the DRC's first office on the top floor of 222 Grays Inn Road. Over time, the DRC would have four main offices – in London, Manchester, Edinburgh and Cardiff – with good standards of disability access and, at its maximum, a cadre of 220 staff. But that December the rather unsatisfactory Grays Inn Road office was the only one, and Bob Niven and his PA were the sole employees (supported by a handful of staff loaned by other Departments). This presented something of a challenge, as the government had announced that the DRC would be fully open for business by April the following year. I agreed with Bob the plans for the organisational structure and initial staffing of the DRC, and under his leadership an urgent recruitment process through open competition began.

It was something of a high-pressure scramble, but the DRC was launched on 25 April 2000. It received a highly positive profile in the print and broadcast media, and was for example the lead item on BBC TV and radio for much of the day. There was a well-attended launch event where both I and the Minister, Margaret Hodge, spoke and gave interviews. Appearances count for much, and we openly assured the Minister and the outside world that the DRC was truly "open for business".

Meanwhile, on the same day, the recruits to our casework and legal teams were completing their initial training in Manchester. Given the tight timing for advertising the jobs, interviews, selection and serving out notice periods, the DRC only had some 40 employees that day (rising to 60 soon afterwards). But already over a third were disabled people, a proportion which remained pretty constant thereafter and which was high in comparison with most employers and all public bodies. Moreover, crucially they were concentrated in senior and middle level posts, not clerical or administrative jobs. From these relatively modest beginnings, the DRC progressively gained momentum and made its impact. We were under way!

The DRC faced a huge task. Its remit covered all of Great Britain. The DRTF had reported that disabled people were among the most disadvantaged groups in society, and this was confirmed by official statistics and the everyday experience of many of us. Moreover, the DRC Act required the Commission to pursue a welcome but wide-ranging set of goals: to tackle discrimination against disabled people; to promote equal opportunities for them; to disseminate good practice; and to keep the legislation under review and make recommendations to Government. Discrimination (intentional or otherwise), prejudice, and physical and other barriers working against disabled people, all remained common. And there were widespread suspicions that the DRC would prove either inimical to the interests of employers and providers of services or – conversely – ineffective, bureaucratic and unduly influenced by Government, despite its independence in statute.

On the other hand, there were important helpful factors at work. Many people had been involved in the campaign for a Disability Rights Commission and the commitment to it in the Labour Manifesto. Public opinion tended to be sympathetic when confronted with the disadvantages faced by disabled people. The DRC's successful launch evoked a positive response in the media and more widely. Governments, of course, want their policies and other initiatives to succeed, and Labour was in power throughout the DRC's life. Successive waves of new disability legislation were to follow. In addition to the employment provisions of the Disability Discrimination Act (DDA) which were already largely in force, there was a timetable over the few years for phasing in its other provisions (including crucially on access to goods and services). There was too the prospect of legislation on other matters highlighted by the DRTF. It was also a time of growing public expenditure (exceptionally for a public body, the DRC's annual budget more than doubled to £23 million within four years). It was the DRC's task to take advantage of these factors through the most effective application of our powers and services and through providing overall concerted leadership.

I had chaired the first meeting of the commissioners in December 1999 and an early decision was to define the overall goal of the DRC as "A society where all disabled people can participate fully as equal citizens". The Commission soon afterwards also committed itself to the mission of "Making rights a reality". And throughout its existence, the Commission was strongly guided by the social model of disability. That is, disability is not to be regarded as an object of pity or charity or as being a type of medical problem. Rather the onus is on society to remove the various types of barriers – physical and others – that prevent people with impairments from having a full and independent life.

The Commission met monthly for over a year until the level of business allowed us to move to meeting every two months. There was a particularly intensive period of work in the early months, with decisions on plans, priorities, strategy, positioning the DRC, services, standards and governance to name just a few. But the volume remained high, with the balance of activity also including for example promoting those waves of new legislation as well as monitoring and learning from DRC services and initiatives.

The Commission was provided with papers on agenda items by the senior managers. I was keen that the papers should be concise and to the point, and generally they were. But the key papers did not always escape Bob's knack, as a former civil servant, of supplementing them with sizeable annexes! Two main committees were established with membership drawn from the Commission: the Legal Committee (on which more later) which I chaired, and the Audit Committee, chaired by John Hougham. John performed this task admirably and, together with Bob and the finance team, ensured for example that the DRC's accounts were never qualified by the National Audit Office and no issue was ever raised by the Public Accounts Committee.

After the early months the Commission's meetings were rotated between the DRC's four offices. This had the benefit of enabling the staff there and commissioners to meet in person. The night before out-of-London meetings, commissioners usually met for a meal, and this enabled informal exchanges of views, news and knowledge relevant to the next day's agenda and beyond. The conversations could range widely; for example, one of the commissioners – who had for a time taught philosophy at Swansea University – regularly provoked some of us into a debate on such subjects as early versus late Wittgenstein. The reader must trust me that, despite what one might immediately think, such conversations stimulated much good humour and engagement (even if not always total comprehension among the rest of us).

Further entertainment was provided one night when the commissioners were staying at a hotel next to Edinburgh zoo. The fire alarm went off at around 3 am and all the guests gathered in the car park, but despite the difficulties which such happenings can cause for disabled people, all the commissioners and DRC staff were safe and sound. We were moreover entertained by the zoo animals. Woken by the noise of the alarms and the floodlights in the car park, they engaged in a prolonged outburst of whooping, roaring, howling and such like. In the end it proved a false alarm (rumour was that the night chef had triggered it by making himself some toast), and we all trailed back to our rooms at 4 am or so. However, as it was June, dawn came very early and triggered a similar, wakening outburst from the direction of the zoo. I felt that the Commission's meeting that day was possibly a little more subdued than usual.

Preparing for and chairing meetings of the

Commission and the Legal Committee, and
attending meetings of the Audit Committee, took
up a considerable portion of my time. My terms of
appointment said the role of Chair would require
four days of my time per week. It is, however, a
truth universally to be acknowledged that such
statements about public appointments are invariably
an understatement. There was, moreover, no such
thing as a wholly typical week. But in addition to
Commission and Committee meetings, there would
be travelling from Liverpool to London and back
each week; speaking engagements; involvement in
a key DRC working party (for example on a Code
of Practice); liaison with stakeholders and individual
commissioners on specific issues; discussions with
staff on emerging proposals for publicity initiatives,
participating in campaigns or major policy initiatives;
and a weekly round-up and forward look with Bob.
There would also be media interviews from time
to time, and some evenings were taken up with
receptions given by disability and other organisations.
And I still had the flat at Broadwater Farm as my
London home base.

By this time I had acquired a specially-adapted
Mercedes people carrier for my travel – a far cry from
the invalid car and Mini of my earlier days, and a big
improvement. It was spacious for manoeuvring within
the vehicle, made loading and unloading my sizeable

electric wheelchair relatively simple, and had welcome features such as power-assisted steering, automatic gears and easy-to operate brakes. It was portrayed as "state of the art", but this did not prevent the occasional breakdown or a part going wrong. There was however a downside in comparison with the invalid car and the Mini – the repairs could only be made by specialist firms, and the bills were far higher.

An important part of the Chair's role was to help maintain good relations with Ministers (not the same thing as always agreeing with them!) The DRC was well served by its sponsor Secretaries of State, David Blunkett, Andrew Smith and – after sponsor responsibility switched from DfEE to the Department of Work and Pensions (DWP) – Alan Johnson and John Hutton. More direct contacts were the so-called "Junior Ministers" in those Departments – the Parliamentary Under Secretaries of State – with whom Bob and I would have round-up meetings every six months or so.

Margaret Hodge proved a real stalwart in the DRC's early years; if Margaret said she would get something done within Government, she did so despite the major pushing and shoving that could be involved. After DWP assumed the sponsor role, Maria Eagle also proved a strong ally, and her successor Anne McGuire was similarly keen to be helpful. More frequent liaison and contacts with officials were primarily conducted by Bob, although the two of us would have round-up meetings with them every two to three months. Those meetings were generally convened by the most senior officials with responsibility for the sponsorship function (among these at DWP was Don Brereton, who later went on to be a first-rate CEO at Motability), and included members of the sponsorship team itself.

It was helpful that many in the team had also been involved in the passage of the Disability Discrimination and DRC Acts, had been part of the DRTF Secretariat and had come over to DWP from DfEE. As it happened, in his previous career Bob Niven had worked extensively with those members of the team as well as with two more senior colleagues elsewhere who went on to be Permanent Secretaries at DWP during the DRC's lifetime. And while I'm mentioning the stratosphere, Prime Minister Tony Blair agreed to a couple of face-to-face meetings at 10 Downing Street and both he and his wife Cherie participated in DRC events.

The DRC's relations with Ministers and the sponsor Department were good and professional, but not cosy. The regular meetings and contacts made for openness and trust. The government respected the DRC's ability to deliver (especially on assisting the effective implementation of the disability rights legislation) while also keeping (consciously, just) within its budgets. Over time, Ministers received consistently favourable comments about the DRC from Parliamentarians, disability organisations, employer and business bodies as well as the public. Critics of the DRC had argued that the Commission could not be truly independent, given that Government determined its budget, formally appointed the commissioners and had to approve the DRC's three year Strategic Plans. In the event, the government did not lean on the DRC to do things it would rather not or generally cause us other major difficulties.

That did not mean the DRC did not have arguments with Ministers. For example, firms with 25 or fewer employees were initially exempt from the employment provisions of the DDA. In 2002 we learned (by accident) that the government had decided not to repeal the exemption as it had been expected to do in a few months' time and that no date for repeal was in sight. No good reason was given for the decision, which was a bad blow for disabled people. Nor did it reflect well on the government's commitment to disability rights or on the DRC's reputation for effectiveness. There was some coverage of the disagreement in the press and a number of commissioners urged that the DRC should publicly be critical of the government's position. I felt that would be counterproductive, especially as it was almost certain that our sponsor Ministers had on this occasion been overruled by colleagues. Instead, the DRC issued a press release whose tone was as much in sorrow as in anger, and embarked on major lobbying of Ministers (in which we were joined by a number of disability organisations and other allies). The repeal was enacted a year or so later.

A further example arose when the sponsor Department was pressing for wording in a Code of Practice which would have enshrined an interpretation of a DDA provision which was at odds with its phrasing and intent, and which would have again worked to the significant detriment of disabled people (such codes in particular set out standards and processes which had in effect to be observed or equalled by defendants in cases under the DDA.) As chance would have it, I had to raise this particular issue at my first meeting with the new Minister, Angela Eagle, and to emphasise that the Commission felt so strongly on the point that we would if necessary take her and the Department to court – perhaps not the best way of getting our relationship off to a good start. It was agreed that officials would discuss the matter further, and the eventual Code reflected the DRC's view. Such disagreements were however the exception.

I have mentioned that the DRC Act gave the DRC a wide range of powers and functions, some of which were additional to those available to the EOC and CRE. At early meetings of the Commission we spent considerable time deciding on how best to deploy those powers and functions and which services the

DRC would provide. My aim was that the DRC would wherever possible use the power of argument and persuasion, but where necessary the argument of power (ie the use of our legal enforcement powers).

The DRC's Helpline, in conjunction with our website, provided the first port of call for disabled people seeking information and initial advice on their rights and whether they had been unlawfully discriminated against. But it also provided information on the law and their statutory duties to employers, providers of services and their advisers. Whenever relevant, the Helpline also directly fulfilled requests for publications.

The Helpline met a major need: on average it received some 100,000 contacts each year (750,000 over its seven and a half years). In total the website received four million visitor sessions. Controversially in the eyes of some, the Helpline was contracted out to a private company, SITEL (they had operated a far smaller publicly-funded disability helpline previously) although their own staff were supplemented by a handful of DRC employees to help assure quality and to deal with the more complex enquiries. The Helpline was a major asset and success, handling far more enquiries than the (in-house) helplines of the EOC and CRE and gaining the top awards of the Telephone Helplines Association and the Customer Contract Association.

Winning awards and high commendations from authoritative third parties became a bit of a habit of the DRC – including several awards for our communications, services, legal work and library. The quality of work and standards achieved by the DRC staff was high and not infrequently outstanding.

The DRC also provided a limited casework service to support disabled people with complaints that had the potential to become full legal cases in the tribunals and courts; a frequently used conciliation service through externally contracted experts for individuals and providers in dispute over access to goods, services and premises; and good practice advice and information for employers and providers via an in-house team.

The Commission also approved the considerable effort and resources that were put into communications campaigns and promotional materials of all kinds.[12] Given our other spending priorities, the DRC budget did not permit sustained generic advertising campaigns in the media. But there were a number of targeted campaigns, particularly on the introduction of new legislation, and as part of the DRC's later strategy to "Close the Gap" between the experiences of disabled and non-disabled people in key sectors of

12. Many of these, together with an extensive range of DRC reports, codes, plans, speeches and other documents about the DRC, can be found at the electronic Archive maintained by the Centre for Disability Studies at the University of Leeds.

the economy and society. Many of these campaigns were GB-wide, while others were specifically tailored to Scotland and Wales.

I and the commissioners pressed consistently for the outstanding parts of the DDA to be introduced and for further new legislation, and the period 2000-2007 saw very substantial advances. In addition to the end of the exemption for small firms, the law on disability and in relation to employment was strengthened further in 2004 and through the widening of the definition of disability in 2005. Far-reaching provisions on education were introduced in 2002, 2005 and 2006. The hugely important Part 3 of the DDA, on access to goods, services and premises, came into force in 2004.

In 2006, following much work by the DRC, the Disability Equality Duty took effect, requiring all public sector bodies to pro-actively assess the risk of disability discrimination across the range of their services and functions and to take the necessary anticipatory steps to prevent discrimination occurring. Such legislation was of course of major benefit to disabled people and their rights, and the Labour Administrations of the time deserve much credit for it. Since then there have been few examples of further progress but instead considerable reverses. The DRC accompanied each wave of legislation with Codes of Practice, guidance and publicity campaigns, prepared in close consultation with all the various interests and groups. This also provided opportunities to underline more general messages about the disadvantages and barriers faced by disabled people as well as the gains that result for them, the economy and society at large in removing them.

"Close the Gap" focused on employment, education, transport together with access to goods and services, and health and independent living. The gaps were defined in terms of indicators such as employment and income levels, education and participation rates, confidence in taking public transport journeys, accessibility in the built environment, and health and care outcomes. In each case the DRC's efforts were focused on securing a range of intermediate steps, including effective legislation, raised awareness and the spread of good practice. My own participation centred largely on the launch events in each sector and on key conferences and public events. These sectoral initiatives focused on measurable outcomes for disabled people, and enabled the DRC 'Heineken' (and me) to reach parts of society we would not otherwise have reached, at least not so extensively.

The DRC's "arguments of force" were the product of its legal strategy and its implementation, led primarily by the Commission's Legal Committee. At the end of the Commission's life, a series of leading experts in the field of disability and discrimination law contributed to a review of all aspects of the DRC's legal work.[13] The contributions were informative and complimentary, and the overall assessment was probably best expressed by Michael Rubenstein, a highly regarded if tough commentator and publisher on discrimination issues: he wrote that it was "generally agreed the DRC has been a great success story. A lot of this is due to the outstanding leadership and excellent staff, but it is also, in no small part, due to the Commission's legal strategy."

The commissioners on the Committee did indeed do an outstanding job, strongly supported by probably the leading discrimination lawyer in the UK, Robin Allen QC, and by the DRC's immensely able Legal Director Nick O'Brien and his admirable team. The Committee approved the legal cases that the DRC would take to Court (an average of 55 a year, well in excess of those taken by the other Equality Commissions and with a high rate of success) or otherwise become involved in. They included an emphasis on cases of particular hardship or outrageous discrimination. But the real key was quality not quantity. We focused on cases that were going to the higher courts, where binding precedents on major issues would be set.

---

13. "DRC Legal Achievements 2000-2007", Disability Rights Commission 2007

We would also quite frequently intervene in cases not on behalf of the appellant but effectively as *amicus curiae* (a friend of the court – an impartial adviser), tendering our views to the judges on the meaning and interpretation of the law itself – this was welcomed by the judiciary. In these ways we helped to "shape" the general application of the law and set the framework for individual decisions. To an extent we acted as guardians of the spirit of the legislation. We also successfully drew on the Human Rights Act in support of disability cases.

Key legal victories included those against the Royal National Theatre Board, which established that the justifiable grounds for failing to make reasonable adjustments for a disabled employee were very narrow; against Fife Council, establishing that the duty to make reasonable adjustments can include positive action in favour of the disabled person; against a leading healthcare firm, in the first DDA case considered by the then highest Court, the House of Lords, establishing that discriminating against a disabled person after the end of their employment contract (in this instance through the giving of references) was unlawful; and against a county council, establishing that constructive dismissal was covered by the DDA. The cases and interventions overall covered a wide range of sectors, circumstances and provisions of the legislation. We could have wished for more, but a number of potentially important and high-profile cases were settled by the parties before finally coming to court.

There were further strings to the DRC's "argument of force" bow. We conducted three formal investigations, whose recommendations were legally binding on the organisations in question. They were on access and inclusion concerning the Worldwide Web, on health inequalities and on the "standards of fitness" required for entry into the teaching, nursing and care professions.

In the latter part of the DRC's life, we also entered into "voluntary binding agreements" whereby the organisation in question, in lieu of being taken to Court, agreed to implement an action plan to end the ways in which the DRC had identified that it discriminated against disabled people. The DRC could provide advice on implementation, and the organisation was liable to be taken to Court if it did not implement the plan. This non-confrontational approach proved attractive to a number of employers and service providers and in the limited time during which they were available, a dozen agreements were entered into, including in the higher education, retail, hotels, and sports and leisure sectors.

I myself almost became the subject of a high-profile case. Ryanair, citing my (lightweight, foldable) wheelchair, refused me access to the plane for a flight I had booked with them, after I had checked in and was waiting on the tarmac. I had to go back to the terminal, and by a mysterious process the media very quickly got hold of the story. Ryanair's action (or perhaps inaction) was almost certainly unlawful, and I was pressed by some commissioners and others to take a case against the company. I decided on balance not to do so, as to start the case was likely to be portrayed elsewhere as inappropriate use of my official position. Fortunately, Ryanair kindly played into our hands by taking similar discriminatory action against another wheelchair user. The DRC supported his case, which went against the company; it then had significant damages to pay.

My Ryanair experience led to two entertaining developments. In the light of the publicity on my incident, the Chairman of a major rival low fare airline phoned me personally to offer to pay the DRC's (or my) legal expenses if we took a case against Ryanair. Regretfully, I decided this was an offer I could and should refuse. Secondly, Ryanair's Chief Executive, Michael O'Leary, contacted me to discuss the issues and to explore solutions. I had two meetings with Mr O'Leary, who proved to be a distinctively-dressed, personable but tough-minded businessman who expressed a keenness to be of help to the DRC. To be fair, Ryanair did adjust their procedures on wheelchairs, but not I judge as a result of our discussions in London and Dublin. Those meetings ran into the sand, not least because Mr O'Leary seemed to be asking the DRC to help him in his ongoing arguments with the British Airports Authority about airport fees and aircraft slots. The conversations were nonetheless reasonably genial, even when, given Mr O'Leary's interest in horses, I asked what he would do if one of his was injured (in effect disabled). He replied "I'd have the fe....g thing shot"!

So despite the hard work, and the distressing experiences of disabled people which consistently came to the DRC's attention, my job as Chair was enjoyable and deeply satisfying. Morale and commitment among the commissioners and staff remained high throughout the DRC's life. And I even got to dress up from time to time.

In 2005, at the invitation of the University's Vice Chancellor, Baroness Hale – who contributed significantly to helpful decisions on disability as a judge and became a member of the Court of Appeal – I was awarded an Honorary Doctorate of Laws by the University of Bristol. In 2008 I was invited to join the Worshipful Company of Wheelwrights (whose charitable priorities included improved access for disabled people and their children) and that in turn led to my becoming a Freeman of the City of London. There are in fact many Freemen (I understand some 1800 people join their ranks each year) and it is not a tightly closed or exclusive group. Nonetheless, the list of Freemen does include some highly-distinguished people in the arts, sciences and public life, people whom I would regard as some way above my league. It was therefore somewhat of a disappointment to me that I did not get to meet such personalities as the actor Michael Caine and perhaps especially the equally renowned (and quite incidentally also glamorous) Joan Collins.

The highlight followed in the shape of an impressive letter from Buckingham Palace in 2006, in effect asking if I would have any objection to becoming a Knight, Sir Bert Massie. I had been fortunate enough to be awarded the OBE in 1984 and the CBE in 2000, and on those occasions too I did of course feel very considerable personal pleasure and pride. However such awards also drove home how much I owed to so many others throughout my life, as mentioned in this book and more widely. My wife-to-be Maureen and my mother were present at the ceremony in May 2007, after which we and other family members as well as friends and colleagues went for a very pleasant, cheery and prolonged lunch. I never in fact asked my mother, but I wonder if, when Prince Charles dubbed me with the royal sword at Buckingham Palace, she was thinking in contrast of the moment close to sixty years previously when my grandmother had to be eased with a helping hand on her backside into the cab of the lorry on Stanley Street in Liverpool which would take me, a small baby with the symptoms of polio, to Myrtle Street Hospital.

The next chapter details the onset of the Equality and Human Rights Commission and my experience as a commissioner there. The announcement of the new Commission and so the impending demise of the DRC could have constituted a hammer blow to morale and momentum at the DRC, among commissioners and staff. In practice, although of course a significant concern, it did not. There was much still to do to ensure the successful implementation of the stream of new legislation and there was no let-up – rather the reverse – in the demand for the DRC's services and legal action. And there was, too, the task of seeking to ensure continued priority for disability in the emerging EHRC and ensuring that the struggle for the rights of disabled people was sustained.

And what of the impact of the DRC? It is not for me to pontificate on this. But independent surveys indicated high regard for the DRC and its work among stakeholders. The Archive at Leeds University includes a further range of works describing and evaluating what the Commission did and achieved. The most comprehensive of these is the 2007 report by the independent Office of Public Management entitled "Evaluating the Impact of the Disability Rights Commission". At 340 pages, it is certainly the most comprehensive evaluation of any equality body in the world, and few other public bodies can have been similarly analysed. It addresses the full range of DRC activities, provides significant comments and insights and poses – but does not endorse – the important question of whether the DRC might have had an even greater long-term impact if it had been more aggressive and sought a higher public profile. Personally I do not believe that would have been the case. But I am content to rest on its overall conclusion that "The DRC was a highly active Commission in its seven years and achieved a great deal."

Towards its closing date of 30 September 2007, the DRC held an awayday in London for all staff and the commissioners. The 220 or so people present made a stark contrast with that near-empty office on Gray's Inn Road that I had first entered in December 1999. Now there was a constant positive buzz and much good humour. Immediately after the main business of the day, photographs were taken of everyone assembled together. The photos show literally all of us smiling and happy. Much had indeed been achieved. The DRC had been a fine experience.

Chapter 10
Inside the Equality and Human Rights Commission

On 1 October 2007, with a metaphorical fanfare of trumpets, the Equality and Human Rights Commission (EHRC) opened its doors to the public, proclaiming its vision was "A Britain at ease with all aspects of its diversity, built on fairness and respect for all". Its birth followed a gestation period so long that no mammal could have survived if its offspring were so dilatory in arriving.

In the 1990s there was growing anger that some people were protected in law against discrimination but others, who also faced discrimination, were not. The Equal Opportunities Commission (EOC) had been

created in 1975 to promote gender equality, and the
Commission for Racial Equality (CRE) had followed in
1976. The Disability Rights Commission (DRC) in 2000
was the new kid on the block, but its creation gave
renewed hope to other groups that sought protection.
These included older people, religious and faith groups
and people of various sexual orientations. None of the
existing Commissions had a mandate to consider their
needs.

Pressure to extend equality laws came from
groups representing those seeking protection and
also from activists in the field of human rights who
saw the limitations of legislation that considered only
equality issues. There was also an important European
dimension. The European Union was investigating
whether protection from discrimination in the provision
of goods and services should be extended to the
excluded groups, and concluded it should.

Article 13 of the Treaty of Amsterdam 1997, and the
Race Directive and Framework Employment Directives
that followed it, influenced the European Commission.
Then came the Equal Treatment Directive in 2006,
which covered gender discrimination. In the UK these
were implemented through regulations rather than by
primary legislation, such as Acts of Parliament, and
there was no attempt to go further or do more than
the Directives required. Sir Bob Hepple argued that
without the European Directives it is unlikely domestic

legislation would have been introduced.[14]

Sir Bob was to play a significant role in the creation of the EHRC. When the Labour Government was elected in 1997, he and Lord Lester proposed that equality legislation should be reviewed. Although the government did not see this as a priority, it saw value in such a review and Sir Bob obtained sufficient funding from voluntary bodies for a one-year review. The result was the Cambridge Report.[15] It recommended a new law to unify equality legislation so all groups were included and a new human rights and equality commission be created. The three current commissions would merge into the new one.

This rang alarm bells when we at the embryonic DRC read a draft of the report towards the end of 1999. If the government accepted the Report, the DRC would be killed before it emerged gurgling from its cradle. The DRC argued that disability discrimination was different from other types of discrimination and if the DRC were prevented from doing its work there would be outrage amongst disabled people.

Colin (later Lord) Low was a DRC commissioner and a member of Hepple's committee. I spoke to him

---

14. Hepple, Bob, The New Equality Act in Britain, The Equal Rights Review Vol 5, 2010. The Equal rights Trust, London.

15. Hepple, B., Coussey, M., Choudhury, T., *Equality: a new Framework: Report of the Independent Review of the Enforcement of UK Anti-Discrimination Legislation*, Oxford, Hart Publishing, 2000.

and pointed out that whatever the merits of Hepple's report I would be unable to support it publicly unless it recognised that the DRC needed more time. As a result of his intervention and that of others, Hepple and his colleagues agreed to amend the report so it stated the DRC should have five years of independent life before becoming part of the new proposed commission. This was a reasonable compromise and I welcomed the report as helpful.

The proposed new commission was not the main or even most important part of the Cambridge Report. It drew attention to the inconsistency in the way Britain had enacted equality legislation and how some groups had wide protection while others enjoyed only partial or no protection. The case for new, consistent legislation was strong and Sir Bob's report was well received. As new groups of people with specific characteristics or, as they were called, equality "strands", were to be covered and the report recommended that stronger human rights measures should also be enforced, there was a strong case for a new human rights and equality organisation to promote and enforce the current and proposed laws. The phrase "equality strands" was shorthand for identifying the particular groups such as gender, age, sexual orientation, race, religion or belief system, or disability. To this list would be added the new strand of human rights.

The Equal Opportunities Commission saw value

in this approach and was always positive about the creation of the new Commission and its own functions being absorbed. I suspect that part of the reason for this was the hope of more resources being devoted to gender equality, as the EOC's budget was small compared to those of the CRE and DRC. The Commission for Racial Equality was less convinced. So were organisations like Black Vote, which had doubts about the effectiveness of the CRE but took the view that "at least it's ours".[16] The stance of the DRC was discussed in Chapter 9, but the view of most disability organisations was clear: they wanted the DRC to remain and saw dangers of its work being diluted by becoming part of a generic commission, although some organisations saw value in closer working with other strands.

It soon became clear that the government did not propose to implement all of Sir Bob Hepple's recommendations, or at least not urgently. However, it did propose to create a single Equality and Human Rights Commission and my job, therefore, was to protect the work the DRC was doing. To enable it to create a new Commission the government would need a new Act of Parliament. This created an opportunity to influence the legislation, so it would require the new Commission to give the same attention to disability

---

16. Conversation between author and Simon Wolley, Operation Black Vote

issues as the DRC. Alternatively, should the DRC campaign to be kept as a separate Commission, especially as it was so new? Whatever position we took at the DRC, we were short of friends as the growing group of supporters for the proposed Commission were eager to ensure that no particular strand had special treatment.

In Parliamentary debates and in the various meetings of interested organisations, the growing and increasingly firm view was that the new Commission should not be organised with different departments catering for different groups of people. A "strand-based" approach was presented as the old way of identity politics in which different groups fought for their own interests and did not identify the common good. In the brave new world all the strands would work together to end discrimination and promote human rights. I was never convinced that this Utopian world existed or would exist, but I was part of a minority. It was as fictional as Huxley's original.

Legislation was on its way and the DRC needed to influence it before it became engraved in stone. It is much easier to change pending legislation before it is written than to change it after it becomes law or appears in a Bill. At the DRC we developed a "federal model" that we thought would work. Under this model the backroom functions would be done collectively. Human rights covered all strands and needed a cross-strand approach. The other strands would have small teams working on strand-specific issues but would come together where an issue affected more than one strand. This would enable the disability strand to deal with issues specific to disabled people, such as access to buildings and transport for those with mobility impairments or easy-read information for people with learning disabilities. Some issues would also affect older people, so the age strand would be involved. This thinking failed to win support outside the DRC. People who did not understand disability could not see why disabled people should be treated differently. It was argued that all strands should be combined to form a unified organisation.

At the DRC we decided to campaign for a statutory disability committee to be included in any Parliamentary Bill. At least half the members would be disabled, and this would help ensure disability policy was in the hands of disabled people. Again, there was resistance to this from other strands, but I spent a great deal of time talking to Ministers and to officials in the Prime Minister's Policy Unit at 10 Downing Street, one of whom, Carey Oppenheim, a senior policy advisor, was particularly helpful. One Minister, Barbara Roach, had suggested to me that if the DRC wished to remain outside the new Commission she would be prepared to consider that option. This appealed to me and to a minority of DRC commissioners. The majority were in favour of becoming part of the new Commission if we could get safeguards. As a result, the offer was never pursued.

When Jacqui Smith became the Minister dealing with the day-to-day business of framing the legislation, she understood the reasons why the disability agenda was different, and she was willing to meet the DRC at least halfway. Jacqui Smith accepted there should be a Disability Committee chaired by a disabled person. She suggested the Committee should have a life of three years. I said "Jacqui, there is no way I can sell that to disabled people. People are pressing me for at least ten years." This longer time-span was not looked on favourably. Trevor Philips, then chair of the CRE, opposed ten years but was prepared to accept five. Eventually, it was agreed that the Bill would include provision for a statutory Disability Committee.

I knew that whoever was in charge of the new Commission would find this an irritant, because it would influence the administrative structure of the organisation. I was convinced they would abolish it as soon as they could. It would not last a day longer than they had to keep it. I therefore proposed that although the Disability Committee should have a minimum life of five years. The new Commission would not have the power to abolish it but could arrange an independent review and even then the decision whether to retain the Committee or abolish it could only be taken by the

Secretary of State. The Disability Committee therefore became one of three statutory committees the EHRC would be required to establish, the others being a Wales and a Scotland Committee. The mere fact that so much effort was made to ensure a disability presence in the EHRC is just one indication of the fear felt by disabled people that it would not be as effective as the DRC.

While the legislation was working its way through Parliament during 2005, the Civil Service machine rolled into action. An inter-departmental group was established to deal with the setting up of the new equality commission. In such cases one of the first tasks is to find a chairman for the proposed quango. The obvious three candidates were the chairs of the three current commissions. The EOC chair, Jenny Watson, indicated that she did not want the post. The recruitment company spoke to me and I gave the same response. Six years earlier I had joined the DRC when it had just four staff. With the support of a superb management team, led by Bob Niven, the DRC had become an extremely effective organisation of over 200 people. I did not believe I had the energy to start from the beginning to create an organisation that needed to be even better than the DRC. That left Trevor Phillips at the CRE. He had been extremely critical of the proposed commission and its mandate, so he was not the most obvious choice. It was also widely acknowledged that the CRE was not as well run as the other two commissions.

It was therefore surprising when the government appointed Trevor Phillips to chair the proposed Commission. With commendable pragmatism, Trevor now found himself singing the praises of the new body and arguing that all his concerns had been met. Although he seemed an odd choice he had qualities which suggested he was ideal for the role. He had a high public profile and was media savvy. He was well connected to senior members of the Labour government. The Prime Minister, Tony Blair, had invited him to chair an Equality Review that covered the whole of society. This review was published in early 2007.[17] Jenny Watson, chair of the EOC, and I played a small part in this project as co-chairs of the reference group of interested organisations.

When Trevor Philips married, Peter Mandelson had been his best man. Trevor had been an excellent journalist and an accomplished broadcaster and public speaker. There should have been nobody better at selling a message and getting it right. I always thought he would have made a reasonable Government Minister, providing he allowed civil servants to run his department. But management was not his forte – that was the problem. His skill was as the front man.

---

17. **Fairness and Freedom: The Final Report of The Equalities Review. Cabinet Office, London 2007**

I had worked with him from the time he was appointed chair of the CRE in 2003. He could be charming, thought-provoking and amusing. He clearly intended to run the CRE his way and he acquired a reputation for creating policy and informing his Board later. Whatever qualities he has, and there are many, he is not a team player unless the team follows and is loyal to him.

I was able to observe him as chair of what in 2007 became the Equality and Human Rights Commission because the legislation provided for each of the previous or legacy commissions to nominate one person to serve as a Transitional Commissioner on the new body. Even before this, we both attended numerous meetings of the shadow government team to establish the EHRC. The DRC had elected me as Transitional Commissioner and so I became an EHRC commissioner. Baroness Jane Campbell was appointed as a full commissioner. She was then asked to chair the Disability Committee. Nobody better could have been appointed.

Trevor Philips moved from the CRE to chair the EHRC. He took on a tough job. A huge number of groups would have high expectations of what it could achieve and most had their own agendas that they hoped the Commission would adopt.

A newly-appointed chair of a new quango has a number of tasks awaiting them. They need to sit on the appointments panels for recruiting commissioners or board members. A chief executive needs to be appointed, offices need to be acquired, the structure of the organisation planned and staff recruited. Then business plans have to be developed, and so it goes on.

The new Board had its first meeting in December 2006, ten months before the EHRC was expected to open and offer services to the public. Several of the seeds that would later produce bitter fruit were planted and nourished in these early months.

Appointments to public bodies are supposed to be on merit, and to some extent they are. But there is usually also a political and personal dimension. Trevor Philips was a Labour politician with deep links in the Labour Party of the time. One result was that a disproportionately large percentage of the new commissioners had strong trades union or Labour Party links. There is no problem with this providing there is balance. A number of the commissioners were appointed for human rights expertise and some because of their expertise in a particular strand.

The Deputy Chair was Baroness Margaret Prosser, a Labour Peer. I do not know why she was appointed, but it was rumoured at the time that her role was "to keep Trevor in check". If so, she failed miserably. She was however to play an important role within the Commission and became a very loyal supporter of

Trevor Philips. I still cannot decide whether this was a genuine reflection of her views or whether she simply liked her well-paid job and wished to keep it. Whatever the reason, had she taken a different approach I believe many of the difficulties that the Commission later faced might have been avoided. Her background in trades union politics should have enabled her to bring people together.

As the places on the Board were filled, it increasingly contained a highly-skilled and experienced group of people. Some of the best equality and human rights brains in the country were sitting around a table together. As a body we would have been stronger had there been more Conservatives or business people amongst our number. Trevor seemed to acknowledge this by wanting to set up other committees or groups representing industry, which he would chair or be part of. This, of course, starts to exclude commissioners and is divisive. This was very much part of Trevor's management style and it became vividly apparent in some of the early papers which commissioners were asked to approve. On one point the new Board was united. It wanted the new commission to be effective and to make a big impact.

It was for Trevor and his Board to appoint a Chief Executive. Philips approached Bob Niven, then working with me as the CEO of the DRC. It would have been a basic courtesy for Trevor to speak to me about his intention before approaching Bob, but he failed to do so. Bob informed me of Philips' offer and said he had turned it down. I think he would have been a superb CEO of the new Commission, and had it had a different chair he might have been interested in the post. He knew of Trevor's reputation at the CRE and had been bemused at his inconsistency in his position on the EHRC. Although I was pleased to keep Bob at the DRC until it closed, had he moved to the EHRC there is a strong possibility that it would have achieved the success that eluded it.

A senior civil servant from the Foreign Office, Dr Nicola Brewer, was appointed as Chief Executive and took up her post in March 2007. My impression was that she was an extremely able woman. In addition to her administrative skills she was accustomed to working with Ministers with different priorities. These were useful skills to bring to the Equality Commission. One of the difficulties in quangos is that chairs who work for three or four days a week can confuse the roles of chair and chief executive. There is little a competent chief executive will find more irritating than the chair seeking to manage all or part of the organisation rather than dealing with the large strategic issues. It was clear from the early days that Trevor Phillips wanted to surround himself with people he knew and trusted, and he soon built a cabal around himself. Some of this group had followed from the

CRE, and the manner in which they were appointed was later to attract considerable criticism. This model of management usually alienates those not in the inner circle. Dr Brewer was never part of the inner circle. Where a chair and CEO do not have a reasonably good relationship there are bound to be tensions that spread throughout the organisation. And so it came to pass!

Before Dr Brewer's arrival, Trevor Philips wanted the Board to agree its working procedures. This was reasonable. At our second meeting, held in January 2007, commissioners were invited to prove a 51-page document of standing orders. Much of this stated the obvious, such as that meetings would be held at a given address 'or elsewhere' – I jest not! Apart from such revelations, the standing orders also proposed delegating significant authority and freedom of action to the Chairman. Papers to the Commission were to be approved by one of Trevor Phillips' personal appointments from the EOC rather than by the Chief Executive, although at that point there was no CEO. But the rules were being set.[18] Predictably, most of us had severe reservations about this paper and it was rejected. It was an early indication that our collegiate style of operating was already under threat. Unfortunately, the governance structures were imported from the old CRE, which in this respect was

---

18. Paper presented to 2nd meeting of the ERCH Jan 2007.

the most dysfunctional of the old commissions, but it was the structure with which Philips was both familiar and comfortable.

When I joined the Board, I expected to spend most of my time seeking to ensure the Commission was successful and that it protected the interests of disabled people. Instead many of my interventions at Board meetings concerned corporate governance. Trevor Philips was not accustomed to being accountable to a Board and thought it would aid efficiency if he were authorised to make the major decisions that could then be reported to the Board. A number of commissioners seemed content with this but others, including me, believed that we had some personal responsibility for the actions of the Commission and its Chair. This was a constant area of tension, as the Chair sought to assert himself and his views without ensuring those were our collective views and not just his own.

Finding premises for the EHRC should not have been contentious, but that also proved problematic. Trevor wanted the London office to be near Whitehall, so he would be close to Ministers and government departments. He argued that such proximity was essential for such an important Commission. I found this unpersuasive, because in seven years at the DRC, located in London's Grays Inn Road, several miles from Whitehall, I had never been required to be in a

Minister's office within 10 minutes. Such meetings were always planned in advance and if a more urgent conversation with a Minister was necessary it could be done by telephone.

Commissioners were asked to approve a lease on office space in Victoria Street, central London. I argued against this proposal because the building had no parking facilities and would be difficult for disabled people to visit. The proposal was dropped. We should not have even been considering premises that were difficult for disabled people to use. It was an early indication that the new Commission did not understand disability issues.

A decision had to be made whether to utilise the offices of the current commissions or to seek alternative accommodation. The DRC had excellent offices which had recently been refurbished and which could have served as a London base for the Equality Commission, but this was dismissed on the grounds that it would be wrong for any part of the Commission to be in a building occupied by one of its predecessor organisations and linked to a specific strand. This logic resulted in significant unnecessary expenditure in equipping new offices. It was also an argument conveniently forgotten when offices used by the old Commissions in Manchester were taken over for the new Commission.

Eventually, the Commission made its London home

at 3 More London Place, close to Tower Bridge. It is difficult to believe the money spent on renting space in this prestigious and swish building could not have been better spent on serving the people for whom the Commission had been established. This building provided views over Tower Bridge and inside it was possible to gaze into the well-furnished offices of other tenants as they oiled the London cash machine.

Both Trevor Philips and Dr Brewer were based on the same floor in the London premises, and great care was taken by the estates staff to ensure their offices were an identical size. Despite the cash spent on equipping this building, when the Coalition Government came to power in 2010 they insisted the EHRC should move to more modest premises.

Brewer's arrival as CEO in March 2007 resulted in immediate improvements, and by June the quality of papers presented to the Board had improved, but the leadership of the Board was still causing me concern. Given the history of the Commission and its relatively limited powers on human rights it was understandable that equality issues were more to the fore than human rights, but one of the justifications for establishing the new commission was to promote human rights. At least two commissioners were recognised experts in human rights, Professor Kay Hamilton and Professor Francesca Klug. I was therefore surprised to receive a phone call from Philips inviting me to be the lead commissioner on human rights. Such an appointment could be viewed as a snub to two people who were more knowledgeable that me. Before accepting I phoned them both to seek their opinion. They encouraged me to accept, but we all knew the Chairman had got this wrong and it was a snub.[19] This type of behaviour eventually resulted in them both resigning from the Commission a couple of years later.

A major task facing Dr Brewer was to ensure that staff were appointed. Staff from the three legacy commissions could transfer to the EHRC, although not necessarily in their old posts. Although many chose not to, there were sufficient people who wished to do so to create a credible Commission, but they had to be interviewed and departments established. It was a time-consuming task made more complex by the determination to avoid strand-based structures. This resulted in some staff from the former Commissions who had specific skills and knowledge having those attributes discounted. In addition some new people were appointed to senior positions. Salaries were much higher than the legacy commissions had offered.

One of the early tasks was to appoint chairs for the three statutory committees, meaning those that the Commission was required to establish under the

---

19. Paper 08.03 presented to 8th Board meeting, Roles and Responsibilities. July 2007

provisions of the Equality Act 2006. Baroness Jane Campbell had been appointed as a commissioner. Baroness Campbell is disabled, and she was and remains a tireless campaigner. Within the DRC she was one of the first to see value in the creation of EHRC, and she argued for the DRC to be positive about it and to help make it successful. As chair of the EHRC Disability Committee, she put together a good committee and was fortunate that Neil Crowther, who had been Head of Policy at the DRC, was appointed as the Disability Programme Director. He was an excellent choice but there was just him and later an assistant. It had a tiny budget of £200,000, which inevitably limited what could be achieved. Baroness Campbell fought hard for additional resources and staff, with some positive results, but no general would have gone into battle so poorly equipped with troops and resources.

The main issue was the obsession with demonstrating that in the new world the EHRC would not engage with issues that affected only one group of people, such as disabled people. The other two committees the Commission was required to establish, one in Scotland and one in Wales, had offices established in their respective countries and directors were appointed, significant budgets allocated and significant responsibilities delegated. This was denied to the Disability Committee, which had a small budget

and just a handful of staff allocated to it. One of the
commissioners, Ziaudddin Sardar, circulated a paper
drawing attention to this anomaly, but it did not result
in action.[20] A direct consequence was that disabled
people received a much inferior service to that the
DRC provided. The EHRC was trapped in part by the
flawed ideology that all work must involve at least two
strands. This nonsense was later quietly dropped so
that issues that had been the responsibility of the EOC
could be considered. If low pay for women is the issue,
it is confusing to include groups for whom it is not an
issue.

This view influenced the EHRC's business plan.
It was heavily infected by the then belief that its work
should not concentrate on the needs of specific
"strands" of people, such as older people or gender
issues, but that it should seek work that could apply to
more than one group. Policy teams did not specialise
in any one group but were generic. This policy was
fraught with problems, because the legal rights
different people had were based on specific criteria
such as disability, gender or sexual orientation. Part of
the reasoning for the approach adopted was the view
that people had multiple identities. They were male
or female, had an ethnic origin, different sexuality,
different age groups and perhaps had a disability. It

---

20. Comments of the Organogram. E-mail to Commissioners.
Ziauddin Sardar 29 April 2007.

was necessary to support all aspects of the person.
The Commission did not just support individual groups
but everyone in society, because all were protected
by equality legislation. Despite this, it remained
true that most disabled people faced discrimination
because they were disabled, whatever their other
characteristics. This all-inclusive approach was never
going to serve disabled people well, or indeed other
strands.

An important service offered by the DRC was its
helpline. The service was outsourced to a commercial
company, SITEL. The helpline is described in Chapter
9, but it won a number of industry awards for being
customer focused. It would have made sense for the
EHRC to have extended the contract but broaden
it to include all the additional groups. Instead it was
decided to establish an internal helpline and, in my
view, standards dropped.

Some years later the government reduced the
EHRC budget and appointed an external company to
offer a limited helpline service. One of the objectives
the Commission gave itself was that in three years'
time, i.e. by 2010, disabled people should think that
the new Commission was an improvement on the
old ones. Changing the helpline service was one of
the actions that ensured this objective was never
achieved.

There is no doubt that setting up a new commission

is a complex management task, but there was ample time to succeed. In June 2007, just over three months before the EHRC was due to open, the Office of Government Commerce produced a Gateway Review of the Commission's progress. All the significant indicators were classed as red, indicating that urgent action was necessary. It is to the credit of the management team that when the Commission opened it was at least able to offer some services.[21]

When the Commission finally opened to the public in October 2007, many aspects of its work were much improved. In addition to the CEO, Patrick Diamond had joined as Policy and Strategy Director and brought humanity and intellectual rigour to the job. John Wadham, previously with Liberty, became Legal Director. A Legal Committee was established, and I joined it. Trevor Philips chaired it and for the most part it worked well, but within the Board the sense of self-importance grew. We debated which part of Government the Commission should report to. Trevor argued that DWP was the wrong department because it was unaccustomed to dealing with organisations that enjoyed the degree of independence the EHRC enjoyed.[22] This was clearly nonsense, as in those days the DWP was a serious Department. However, there was a valid point as the Commission was concerned

---

21. **Paper presented to the Board at its 7th meeting, June 2007**

22. **Minute 09.6.1 of EHRC Board at its 7th meeting, 20 Sept 2007**

with equality and human rights but within government these were separated and human rights rested with the Justice Department and equality issues moved from one department to another.

We also began to have serious discussions on human rights. I discussed in Chapter 6 why human rights are so important for disabled people. In general terms, human rights give absolute values whereby equality legislation is always comparative. Equality concerns treatment between different groups of people and ensures one group is not treated less favourably. The EHRC was faced with a major limitation contained in the Equality Act 2006. It could only support legal action on human rights if the issue was also linked to equality. It was unable to use litigation to promote an issue that was solely concerned with human rights. What it was permitted to do was promote human rights in general terms, and I was eager that it should do so.

One way it could act was to launch an inquiry into how human rights were or were not being implemented in the UK. A proposal was put to the Commission, but concern was expressed that such an inquiry might be inappropriate.[23] It was agreed to produce a leaflet on human rights.

Eventually an enquiry was set up in 2008. Although we had excellent human rights expertise within the Commission, Trevor Philips wanted to bring in an

23. Minute 09.5/20 of ERHC Board meeting, 20 Sept 2007

external chair for the inquiry. I held the view that he did not wish to major on human rights because the press were so negative about the issue. I therefore feared that he might appoint a crony to ensure the inquiry ran into a cul-de-sac and never found its way out, so it was an agreeable surprise when Dame Nuala O'Loan was appointed. She arrived with an excellent reputation because of her work in Northern Ireland. The lead commissioner was Professor Francesca Klug, and the other commissioners were the chair of the Wales Committee and me.

We saw the Inquiry as an opportunity to develop what would become the EHRC's policy and practice on human rights, which some of us viewed as amongst its most important roles. Its terms of reference were "to inform the Commission's future strategy to give effect to its statutory obligations on human rights under the Equality Act; to assess progress towards the effectiveness and enjoyment of a culture of respect for human rights in Great Britain; to consider how the current human rights framework might best be developed and used; to realise the vision of a society built on fairness and respect, confident in all aspects of its diversity." [24]

Dame Nuala proved to be a perfect chair. We took evidence from a wide range of organisations and

24. **Human Rights Inquiry. Report of the Equality and Human Rights Commission. ERHC July 2009**

some of them took the opportunity to reconsider their own organisation's action in relation to human rights. Asking the right questions acted as a catalyst. Most organisations suggested that the EHRC should be more proactive on human rights and hoped the inquiry would result in a more dynamic approach.

Although the work on the inquiry was stimulating, we were frustrated at lack of support and resources from the Commission, even though the staff appointed to support us were willing and able. There was a sense that whatever our report said we could have no assurance that it would result in action. My dissatisfaction with the leadership of EHRC was growing more intense, and I considered resigning. Dame Nuala encouraged me to stay, at least until the inquiry was published.

At the Board meeting in November 2007, some members expressed concern that the Chair had given a speech on immigration and fairness.[25] This was a contentious speech that was delivered on the anniversary of Enoch Powell's famous "Rivers of Blood" speech – and in the same hotel. It was a publicity masterstroke, but he had not consulted commissioners to see if they agreed with it. After internal protests, Trevor Philips wrote to commissioners setting out his reasons for doing so,

---

25. http://www.telegraph.co.uk/news/politics/1896134/Trevor-Phillips-warns-of-immigration-cold-war.html

but this was after the event. Some of us argued that policy should be agreed by the Board in advance and that it was not acceptable for Trevor to invent policy and attribute it to the Commission, as this put commissioners in the impossible position of being expected to publicly support policies they did not support, and which they had been denied an opportunity to influence during their development. This made nonsense of collective responsibility. There was a sense that Trevor Philips made policy on the hoof and the rest of us were supposed to step into line. It was impossible to stop him using the Commission to project his own views and, the question of whether they were also those of other Commissioners was somewhat hit and miss.

There were other concerns. Staff from the legacy commissions could either transfer to the EHRC or accept redundancy. A number of Trevor's former colleagues at the CRE accepted redundancy and were then recruited by the EHRC to fill vacancies in posts to support the Chair. This was somewhat irregular and the CEO, who, in her role as accounting officer, was accountable to Parliament for the Commission's use of public funds, expressed her concern. One result was that the National Audit Office refused to sign off the Commission's accounts. Trevor claimed it was nothing to do with him but was the responsibility of the CEO. He was skilled at covering himself with Teflon.

Dr Brewer later defended her position by pointing out that the staff were on the payroll when she arrived and she had extended their contracts because of staff shortages.[26]

Trevor Philips had also established a consultancy company, Equate, in which he sought additional work on a private basis. There is no problem with someone doing this, but it becomes one when they chair a public body, especially one in the same subject area. The potential conflicts of interest were obvious and contravened the rules governing public appointments. He could be working for a company or organisation that was subject to regulation or legal enforcement by the Commission. I advised him to withdraw from Equate, but he was reluctant to do so. It was only when the whole thing became public that he acted. But in the meantime, he had put Dr Brewer, the CEO, who had also advised him to sever his link, in an impossible position.

I was not part of Dr Brewer's inner circle so I was not privy to her thinking, but in joining the EHRC she was on unpaid leave from the Foreign Office. In March of 2009 she resigned. The first I heard of this was a conference call chaired by Trevor Philips who explained that she had been offered a "dream job" as High Commissioner to South Africa. I recall saying

26. House of Lords, House of Commons Joint Committee on Human Rights. Equality and Human Rights Commission. Thirteenth Report of the Session 2009-10. TSO 2010.

nothing of any substance during this meeting. It was obvious what had happened and nothing I could say would change it. We also lost Patrick Diamond, one of our senior policy people. We were losing good people and the Commission was, as a result, weaker.

It was clear to me that governance and the style of chairmanship had to be discussed and resolved. The *Daily Mail* was printing negative articles about Trevor Philips' consultancy arrangements, but he argued it was an attack on the whole Commission and not on him personally.[27] That was one way of looking at it! I hoped this could be sorted out internally, and sent an email to Margaret Prosser suggesting we establish an internal group chaired by her as Deputy Chair and comprising the chair of the Audit Committee, Ben Summerskill, Kay Hampton, Baroness Campbell, Jean Drake, the Transitional Commissioner from the EOC and myself. Nothing came of this and instead it was decided that the consultants Deloitte should be hired to review governance. The need to review governance at a cost of over £30,000 just a year after the ERHC was established was damning, and I objected because I thought it the wrong approach. People employ consultants for a number of reasons, many honourable. They are also used to delay decisions, or to provide the answer the organisation already knows but is afraid to act on and seeks external justification.

---

27. http://www.dailymail.co.uk/news/article-1024953/Channel-4-paid-race-chief-Trevor-Phillips-deal-fallout-Big-Brothers-Shilpa-row.html

They sometimes provide the illusion of action. In objecting I outlined what the results would be, and so it came to pass.

I was looking for an analysis of the role of the Chair and commissioners with a focus on accountability and internal consultation. The first draft of the report did discuss some of this, but by the time it reached the Board in May 2009 it had been sanitised. Deloitte's report was mild about the Chair's conduct and referred to the need to clarify the relationship between the Chair and CEO.[28] As we had lost a first-rate CEO, this was hardly a world-shattering insight. Perhaps the greatest understatement was: "There is a perception that the Board has the potential to improve the level of collaboration, trust and consensus-based decision-making within the Board." This neatly suggests that the Board was responsible, whereas the tone is set at the top of an organisation. The report also suggested the Board should be reduced in size, thereby implying the structure was wrong rather than that there was something wrong with the way it was managed. I have sat on many boards larger than that at EHRC, but none so badly chaired.

The response was bureaucratic, with a long paper imposing behaviour standards on commissioners. In fairness, most of them were common sense, but the opportunity to deal with the true issues was lost. Had

28. Summary of the Review Recommendations (Deloitte) and Implementation. May 2009. Paper presented to the Board on 5 May 2009

there been a full review, involving people who knew the problems, the events of a few months later could have been avoided. Dark clouds were gathering, but the leadership of the Commission either could not see them or ignored them.

When Dr Brewer left she created a vacancy for a new Chief Executive. It became clear that Trevor Philips wanted to appoint the Group Communications Director, Kamal Ahmed, an experienced journalist, and not to advertise the vacancy. Concern was expressed that a public body could not appoint a CEO in such a casual manner. I knew that nothing I said would change Philips' mind, but whatever Ahmed's qualities the Commission would face heavy criticism if such a senior appointment was made without advertising the job externally so that it was competitive. The junior minister then responsible for the Commission was Maria Eagle, and I told her of my concerns. The post was then advertised, although it resulted in only a temporary appointment.

One hope some of us had come from the knowledge that Philips' appointment as Chair was soon to end. His term of office ended in autumn 2009. Although he had originally indicated that he would serve only one term it was becoming apparent that he was interested in continuing. Various commissioners spoke to civil servants and ministers to inform them that if he were reappointed there would be resignations. It was clear that a number of people shared our concerns, and this included Ministers and senior civil servants. Baroness Campbell has put it on public record that she spoke to the head of the Civil Service.[29] I had spoken to the civil servant who headed the government Equality Office, now the EHRC's sponsor department, and he seemed to share my view. The Minister ultimately responsible was Harriet Harman. In an informal chat with her at a reception I informed her of my concern, but she seemed uninterested. I suspect that without Harman's support Philips would not have been appointed to a second term.

Harriet Harman announced in July that Trevor Philips would be appointed to serve a second term as chair. Margaret Prosser was reappointed as Deputy Chair, but all other commissioners would be expected to re-apply if they wished to continue.[30] For many of us this was the finally straw. Kay Hampton had resigned after the CEO resigned. Baroness Campbell resigned, but kept her council. Francesca Klug resigned on the same day as me, 18 July 2009. I had only a few months left to serve so my position was not important,

29. House of Lords, House of Commons Joint Committee on Human Rights. Equality and Human Rights Commission. Thirteenth Report of the Session 2009-10. TSO 2010.

30. http://www.standard.co.uk/news/how-did-trevor-phil-lips-get-reappointed-as-equalities-commission-boss-6754534.html

but if I had stayed it would have undermined the position of those who had resigned. If I had continued to the end of my term it would have been used to suggest I disagreed with those who resigned. I supported their views fully and had spoken with them on many occasions.

In my letter of resignation addressed to Harriet Harman giving my reasons, I drew attention to poor corporate governance, which affected the work of the Commission. I was also annoyed that perfectly good Commissioners were expected to reapply if they wanted to serve a second term while Trevor Philips and Margaret Prosser were reappointed despite their record. I wrote:

In addition, the Chairman's conduct in various ways has damaged the Commission's external reputation and standing in the media and among stakeholders. He has now become the constant bad news story over many months, crowding out the EHRC's ability to secure coverage for the key substantive issues to do with equalities and rights in Britain.

I had made it clear over six months before that I did not propose to seek reappointment. I am however saddened that Commissioners have been informed that their appointments will not be renewed and if they wish to continue as a Commissioner they must re-apply. This is an unusual procedure as it is normal

*practice for people to be offered a second term
provided they have performed adequately during the
first term. If they then desire a third term they must
compete with others. Instead, it is rather as though at
Balaklava Lord Cardigan had been re-appointed and
the remnants of the Light Brigade invited to re-apply
for their posts. There are many more sensitive ways
of reducing the size of the Commission if that is the
objective.* [31]

I circulated the letter to a number of people connected
to the EHRC but did not send it to the media. Perhaps
predictably it was quickly leaked, and my comment
referencing Lord Cardigan was widely quoted in
newspapers and magazines.

A few days later the chair of the Audit Committee,
Ben Summerskill, resigned. Including the CEO, who
was also a commissioner, six commissioners had
resigned in a few months. That should have sent out
a message. To misquote Oscar Wilde, to lose one
Commissioner is unfortunate; to lose two is careless.
To lose six?

Naturally, Trevor Philips did not seek to defend
himself in person, but the ever-faithful Margaret
Prosser was sent to do the media round. Like a good
politician, she did not seek to address the major issues

31. **Letter from Author to Harriet Harman MP, Minister for
Women and Equality 18 July 2009**

but instead sought to devalue those who had resigned. On Radio 4's Today Programme she argued that Baroness Campbell and myself were never committed to cross-strand working and just wanted the DRC to be recreated. She went on to say that I had missed a number of Board meetings. The journalists did not know enough to challenge her, but the truth was very different. As I record in Chapter 9, when at the DRC Baroness Campbell argued for merging with the new Commission. She was committed to the EHRC and to cross-strand working. I had done all I could to make the Commission an effective body. There was no chance that the DRC could be recreated. Those working on disability issues had a strong interest in making the EHRC effective.

Baroness Campbell copied to me an email she had sent to Margaret Prosser pointing out that she had been misrepresented by Prosser, who must have known the Baroness's views because she had discussed them with her on the Terrace of the House of Lords. She called on Prosser to withdraw her remarks and apologise. I have no knowledge how Prosser responded.

Had I not resigned, I would have felt a deep sense of disloyalty to those who had. But by resigning I felt I had let down the DRC commissioners who had elected me as the Transitional Commissioner. I sent a full note to them covering some of the ground above, but which included the following paragraph.

There was a very angry meeting of the Commission which I was unable to attend but Jane [Campbell] was there and read out in full an email I had sent on the issue. I was subsequently attacked on the Today programme by Baroness Prosser for missing some Board meetings. Indeed I had, but in the year in question of the 20 days I was committed to working for EHRC, I had worked 39. I put a lot of work into the Human Rights Inquiry in which disability features largely. I was also forming the opinion that what was said at Board meetings was difficult to relate to subsequent actions by the EHRC. I have attended nearly all the monthly meetings of the Legal Committee.[32]

The fact that I had worked almost twice my contracted days was deliberately ignored by Prosser.

There was widespread press coverage of the affairs of the EHRC commission and its strengths and weaknesses, but newspapers had a field day criticising the Commission and the fact that the National Audit Office was critical of its use of public funds. A deeper enquiry was clearly needed, and this came from Parliament.

---

32. Email from the author to former commissioners of the DRC, 22 July 2009

In Parliament most committees comprise members from only one of the Houses, Lords or Commons. Some committees have members from both Houses and one of these is the Joint Committee on Human Rights (JCHR). It decided to launch its own enquiry, and in October 2009 I found myself and other Commissioners who had resigned appearing before the Joint Committee to explain ourselves. These Committees can be intimidating, as the members sit at a horseshoe-shaped table with the chairman at the apex. At the bottom in a row sit the witnesses and behind them are rows of seats for the public. In the middle of the horseshoe sits a stenographer who takes a verbatim record of what is being said. Witnesses are usually invited to make an opening statement and then answer questions.

Baroness Campbell, who had also resigned, made written submission to the JCHR and was not called to give evidence in person. Before the Committee was Professor Francesca Klug, Professor Kay Hamilton, the CEO of Stonewall, Ben Summerskill and me. The Committee seemed to me to make a determined attempt to discover why we had resigned and whether we had given up too easily. We rehearsed and expanded on what we had said previously. Professor Klug was as ever highly principled and chose each word with care. She explained that she had tried on several occasions to persuade Philips to be more collegiate. She pointed out that a number of his more contentious public comments had not been agreed by the Commission but were presented as agreed policy. Margaret Hamilton had worked with Philips at the EOC and had witnessed his difficulty in working with CEOs, and when Dr Brewer resigned she had seen history repeating itself and decided she wanted nothing of it, so she resigned. Ben Summerskill had chaired the Audit Committee but was so concerned at some of the expenditure he did not think he could assure the National Audit Office that finances were controlled, so he felt he could not stay. I concentrated on governance issues. I also said that human rights had not been given a sufficiently high priority within the Commission's work plan. I rather rashly suggested that the Commission was the only organisation able to do such work and was reminded by the chairman that his Committee was also making a contribution. It was a fair point.

Trevor Philips was invited to meet the Committee on a later date and was accompanied by the Legal Director, John Wadham, and two Commissioners, Kay Carbury and Jean Drake, both trade unionists and supporters of Philips. Carbury and Drake claimed that they did not recognise the disunity others and I had identified, and they thought the Commission was well run. Philips defended his role with the skill and finesse of a diplomat. Problems were either the responsibility of others or he had no knowledge of them. He presented himself as a consensual chairman doing a difficult job. Polished though he was, the JCHR were also experts and in a carefully worded report they criticised Philips' reappointment without competition. They also argued that the Commission should have done much more on human rights and the fact that so many commissioners had resigned indicated there were serious problems at the Commission.

Of course, much of this was already water under the bridge. Philips was in post and new commissioners had been appointed. The lasting damage was to the reputation of the Commission and its abject failure to support civil and human rights as it should have done. When established it had had many friends, but it had lost most of them.

When the Cameron Government was elected it wanted to abolish as many quangos as possible and it looked at getting rid of the EHRC. It was saved because the government needed an independent body to be the agency reporting to the United Nations on human rights in the UK. The Commission was saved but its budget was reduced to a little over £20 million, or about the same as the DRC had when it closed. It was later reduced further. Of course, the EHRC has much wider responsibilities.

When Trevor Philips finished his second term as chairman he was replaced by Baroness Onora

O'Neill, a distinguished academic. The number of commissioners was reduced. Its public profile is much reduced at a time when human rights are being abused on a regular basis.

Looking back, I regret that I was part of causing so much damage to the EHRC. In its weakened state it was not in a position to defend itself when the Cameron Government came calling. It is now a sad shadow of what it could be. Despite this it did do some good work. While the Board might have been dysfunctional, excellent staff were doing work that got results.

The Legal Department did some good work in supporting legal cases or intervening in others. Naturally, the early "wins" were inherited from the legacy commissions, as it can take over a year before starting a legal case and resolving it. However, the EHRC can take all the credit for challenging the British National Party. This was largely a Philips initiative, but it was discussed and agreed. The damage this challenge did to the BNP emerged after I had left, but it was the type of strategic action the Commission should undertake.

At the time of writing the EHRC is not serving disabled people as well as the DRC had done. Did we make the wrong decision in agreeing to the merger? Although I was unenthusiastic about the merger at the time, I think those who argued for it might well have been right. Joining when we did created an opportunity to have the disability committee established by law, which gave some protection for this area of work.

When the Committee was five years old in 2013 it was subject to a statutory review. As I predicted, the new leadership of the EHRC wanted to abolish it, but the review rejected its opinion and the government supported this, so the Committee continues until it is next reviewed.[33] Had the DRC remained independent it might have lost good staff to the EHRC, which paid higher salaries.

It is questionable how long the DRC could have remained independent. It merged into the EHRC in October 2007. In May 2010 the Coalition Government was elected and was hostile to quangos like the DRC. It abolished many of them, and it is possible they would have just abolished the DRC. The government was introducing expenditure cuts, some of which convened the human rights of disabled people. It would not wish to fund a body that drew attention to this fact. Alternatively, it could have transferred the function to the EHRC but given disability issues no protection, so that once again people with no knowledge or experience of disability would set disability policy. I suspect the life of the DRC would have been short after the 2010 election.

---

33. Agnes Fletcher, Independent Review of the Disability Committee. EHRC, London 19 July 2013

The challenge for the EHRC is to live up to the
expectations of those who fought for its creation. At
the moment it is a long way from that, but the future is
another day. A report from a committee in the House
of Lords reported in 2016 and demonstrated how
civil rights for disabled people had declined and that
the EHRC was failing to protect disabled people. [34]
Disabled people had argued that the DRC was still
missed. Perhaps in the future we do need a debate
on whether disability issues should be removed from
the mandate of the EHRC and giving to a commission
with a single focus. That is what many disabled people
want.

34. The Equality Act 2010: The Impact on Disabled People,
London, The Stationery Office, March 2016

Chapter 11
Reflections

As my life draws to an end, the inevitable question arises: Did I spend it sufficiently well, or did I miss many unseen opportunities? Would I have been more useful in some other field than disability? It is impossible to know but I followed the paths before me.

I was born into a world in which the support disabled people received was based very much on a medical model, which in some respects reflected the newly-created National Health Service. Even following the war, when the United Kingdom really knew about austerity, there seemed no attempt to starve disabled children of medical or educational resources. The issue that became prevalent during the next 10 or 15 years was how those needs should be met.

There were already organisations either run by disabled people or non-disabled people who were fighting for a better life for those they represented. The definition of disability was relatively narrow. It included people with significant physical, intellectual and sensory impairments. Many of those who would be later recognised as disabled, such as people with dyslexia or autism, did not receive the same degree of attention. Many people who had mental illnesses were not judged to be disabled.

From my teens onwards I evolved into a disability activist. I possessed the primary qualification of being disabled, unable to walk and with weak arms. I was later to discover that such definitions were far too superficial. By the time I was employed by RADAR, I had experience in campaigning and lobbying. Of the major disability organisations in London RADAR was, at the time, the one most involved in campaigning to improve public transport, access provision, education etc. Most of the other major charities did some campaigning but were mainly concerned with provision of services for their members. For example, SCOPE operated a number of schools and residential facilities. The early 1980s, following the publication of the CORAD report, gave us a perfect platform on which to build. It happened to coincide with the creation in the UK of the British Council of Organisations of Disabled

People (BCODP), who argued that none of the major charities had the legitimacy to represent them. In essence their view was that only disabled people could comment and set the agenda for disability issues and organisations should shed their non-disabled staff and members and only permit disabled people to join.

The argument of legitimacy was powerful. What right did non-disabled people have to set the agenda when they had been doing so for many years with such poor results? Although the key people in the various elements of the disability movement knew each other, there were wide variances in views. It is however an indication of the influence BCODP had achieved that although they had no legal authority the large charities did listen to their views, and so did some of the funding organisations. They could not be ignored.

RADAR was seen by BCODP as an organisation for disabled people rather than of them, because it was not controlled by disabled people. In those days, BCODP argued that control normally meant that the constitution needed to require at least 51% of the board to be disabled. When I looked around the board of RADAR we could easily meet that percentage, but it was not contained in the constitution. I also attracted personal criticism as a disabled person working for an organisation not legally controlled by a majority of disabled people. I could easily dismiss this argument because it was not based on what I was doing, merely the position I occupied. I suspect I would have won accolades had I simply resigned my post and condemned the organisation that had employed me. I was convinced that RADAR was doing a great deal of good for disabled people and saw no reason not to remain involved.

The BCOPD attacked RADAR on a number of grounds. I suspect the true reasons included the following. The first was that RADAR was influential and that influence deprived the "disability" movement of influence. It was as though there was a set amount of influence and the more RADAR had the less was available to BCODP and its members. Second, RADAR still received a grant from the government. To some extent this gave the organisation legitimacy, but mostly it gave it financial security. Constant calls for the government to remove this funding from RADAR were made by those organisations that saw themselves as part of the "disability movement". It was many years before this demand was reduced to suggesting that funds should be transferred to organisations "of" disabled people. Thirdly, that RADAR was not fully committed to the disability rights agenda, and rather than supporting disabled people was undermining them. This was a strong allegation but had no substance. There were various views on strategy and tactics.

I can fully understand why the disability movement

chose to attack the major charities. They highlighted the "Big Six" disability charities, most of which employed over 2000 people. At its largest RADAR never employed more than 60. RADAR was hardly one of the Big Six in terms of size, but in campaigning and lobbying terms, it did have a large footprint.

RADAR had over 400 disability organisations in membership with it and held regular regional meetings to obtain their views. As a general rule it received warm support from disability groups across the country. It could of course be argued that the groups were self-selecting, that those who damned RADAR would not attend our meetings. As it developed policies it constantly consulted on them and tested them before arguing for them. I was not operating as a one-man army but as part of an organisation using corporate structures. I therefore resisted the arguments, although there were some I was happy to support. It had to be a good thing if more disabled people were involved in disability organisations. At RADAR there had always been significant numbers of disabled people in positions of influence. But of course, not all disabled people hold the same views.

However, the disability movement grew more influential and as it did so it used its the voice. A great deal of time during the 1980s and 90s was spent fighting a low-level internal war between disability organisations. While we were indulging ourselves, social care was being cut and there were ever-growing pressures on disability benefits.

The organisations supporting direct action and the like became known as the 'Movement' and as it matured it did in my view make some important positive contributions. The first was that it promoted the Social Model in a way that the major organisations had not. The Social Model had been developed by Vic Finkelstein and popularised by Mike Oliver and there are libraries of books written about it, but it is a simple concept. It argues that people might have an impairment, but they only have a disability if society is not organised in accordance to their needs. As an example, a person in a wheelchair approaching a building fitted with a ramp remains impaired, but they are not disabled because they can get into the building. If the ramp is replaced by steps, they can't get into the building and as a consequence are disabled. Disability is therefore a social concept defined by society.

This simple philosophy was immensely liberating for disabled people. Gone were the days when we would accept some responsibility for their impairment and perhaps even feel guilty about it. Instead they could approach the world with confidence, knowing that with good campaigning the world could be changed and the Social Model gave a good agenda of what might be done.

The model also indicated that the reason a person was using a wheelchair was not important and all wheelchair users were united in needing the avoid steps. The cause of their impairment was irrelevant. One consequence was that many more disabled people became disability activists and joined the movement. When the battle for the DDA intensified, they provided many useful soldiers and leaders.

The movement was also very good at mobilising groups of disabled people to fight for better independent living, and a number of legislative changes were a consequence. What became apparent later is that the Blair and Brown governments were extremely supportive of disabled people. Once the Cameron government got elected with its agenda to reduce the size of the state, there came dramatic cuts in social care services and a vicious attack on disability and benefits. The battles of the 1960s and 70s to have incapacity benefit introduced have largely been brushed aside as the government has made it much more difficult for people to claim Employment Support Allowance and has tightened the criteria dramatically. Apart from a few groups such as Black Triangle, which has campaigned well, the disability lobby has not been able to resist these cuts. The thin disability lobby of the 1970s grew in strength in the 80s and 90s, but it is now much weaker. The large charities still exist, and they appear to control the agenda.

RADAR, which had done so much in the 80s and 90s, ran into funding problems and has undergone many changes since. It is now Disability Rights UK, a much smaller organisation fighting on very specific issues and still supporting the Parliamentary All Party Disability Group. The government listens to it, but it and other charities lack the influence they once had.

The Social Model

Although the Social Model played an important role in creating a new perspective from which to view and analyse issues related to impairment and discrimination, it did not always receive the critical scrutiny from which it would have benefited. Part of the difficulty was that if anybody publicly criticised any aspect of the Social Model they were immediately subject to significant personal abuse or attack, and this inevitably led to people accepting the model's status as a deity and not to be questioned.

However, some individuals were courageous enough to question it. In a lecture at City University, London, Lord Low questioned whether in sociological terms it was sufficiently robust to act as a model at all. He also pointed out that in many of its aspects it was not strictly social. Dr Tom Shakespeare, in his book *Disability Rights and Wrongs*, also questioned whether it was sufficiently robust to justify the status it acquired.

I could see the very real liberating effects of the Social Model and how disabled people were using it. It also provided a very simple way of explaining to non-disabled people the principles behind seeking to change a society's infrastructure, rather than concentrating on rehabilitating disabled people. I suspected the main problem was that promoting and defending the model became almost an objective in itself and was often undertaken at the price of work that might have been more productive. Personally, I had been operating Social Model principles most of my life. So had many disability organisations, including organisations "for" disabled people. For example, during the 1980s a great deal of work was undertaken to rewrite building regulations to ensure they required access provisions for disabled people to be included in all new buildings. This was a pure social model, but even then it was impossible to concentrate on only social aspects and to ignore issues related to impairments.

One of the difficulties in determining access in the 1970s was that we lacked adequate definitions of disabled people. By the 1980s it was common ground that although wheelchair users preferred ramps, large numbers of ambulant disabled people preferred low steps. At some point we had to return to considering people's impairments to apply Social Model principals.

All these issues could have been dealt with calmly

and quietly, but they became the topics of heated public debate and frequent attacks on individuals. I seemed to spend far too long in the middle of these storms.

The issue of legitimacy did have another effect. Many of the "Big Six" charities did begin to examine whether they should increase the number of disabled people on their governing bodies. The RNIB discovered it had far more disabled people on its various committees than it realised. It also employed a significant number of disabled people, and I found when dealing with the RNIB on joint policy issues that I was almost invariably dealing directly with a blind person. Indeed, the calibre of the staff it employed enabled it to make significant contributions to developing policy for other impairment groups. It grew into an extremely effective campaigning organisation as well as one that provided services to blind and partially-sighted people.

The notion that to be a disability campaigner you had to be disabled also caused some confusion and raised eyebrows. During the mid-90s battle for what became the Disability Discrimination Act, Victoria Scott, RADAR's Parliamentary Officer, received some marked criticism for not being disabled. It was suggested to me that she should be moved away from the campaign and replaced by a disabled person. I suspect she was one of the people whose contribution did more than most to result in legislation eventually being passed. However, even this was not seen as a positive by some, who thought it would be better not to have any disability legislation, such as the DDA, as it would be better to wait for a Labour Government to introduce the more comprehensive legislation people were demanding. It was quite clear to me that the debate had become ideological to such an extent that people were no longer prepared to think clearly about the issues, and one consequence was that I saw no reason to alter RADAR's position.

While RADAR's regular meetings with our members around the country did enable more mature reflections, the movement's constant attacks meant every position had to be constantly examined and re-examined. I recall attending the Labour Party Conference in 1980. In the 80s I attended all three major party conferences, where I and others from RADAR spoke at various meeting and attended many others. At the conference I was speaking to the Labour MP, Lewis Carter-Jones, who had a long history of raising disability issues in the House. He had said to me that in parliamentary terms it is always a mistake to try to tackle too many topics on a particular occasion. The more that is contained within a Bill, the greater the difficulty the government will have in maintaining control over future amendments that are proposed. The Treasury looks at all legislation from the viewpoint of cost. If it could argue that cost was becoming disproportional or overly expensive, it would mobilise its considerable resources to blocking it. If the Treasury could be brought on side there was a much greater chance of the legislation reaching the statute book.

There is a danger that if Parliament accepts an inadequate Bill it allows the government of the day to argue it is doing a great deal for disabled people while doing relatively little, and this also weakens disabled people's demands for subsequent legislation. The arguments are finely balanced. However, there is no doubt that the Social Model had a profound influence on the major charities and was a useful way of improving the organisations.

In the case of the Disability Discrimination Act, its long genesis and legislative journey seemed to back Carter Jones's point of view. Many of the demands made of subsequent legislation were not contained in Peter Large's CORAD Report and, in fairness to Large, in the early 1980s we lacked the research to frame some of his proposals in legislative terms. For example, he wanted trains to be accessible. This was interpreted at the time as meaning that wheelchair users should no longer need to travel in a cold and dirty guards van, even if they were given a 50% discount for the privilege. But what did he mean by access? In the 1970s British Rail had conceded that on their newest coaches a first-class seat in one carriage could be removed to enable a wheelchair user to travel in their wheelchair. The space had to be booked in advance and as a frequent user of the service I know that in almost 50% of cases, the seat had not been removed and this had to be done at the station while I waited with other rail passengers staring at me as though I was personally responsible for their delay. But even when on the train there was no access to a lavatory that was accessible to a wheelchair user.

In those days most toilets on railways resembled those on airlines and were little larger than upright coffins. One of the campaigns in which I was involved of which I am most proud was designing on-board toilets to be accessible to disabled people, and disability lobbyists received a huge amount of support for this from engineers at British Rail and at the Department of Transport. The conversation then moved on to "should carriages contain better colour contrasting?" to help visually-impaired people, those with some vision although they might not be classified as blind.

Gradually, on this as in taxis, buses etc, a slow, methodical approach gave us the information on which subsequent legislation could be framed. When in 1994 disabled people were chaining themselves to buses on Westminster Bridge in London, it was an important part of the publicity battle, but the essential battle had already been won. This was because work had been under way for many years to define the nature of an accessible bus and whether it was technically possible to build it.

The slow speed of developing and incorporating legislative change into law often means the end result is far better than it otherwise would have been. Certainly this has been the case in disability legislation. Unfortunately, however much thought is put into drafting legislation it will always, sooner or later, need to be amended and that is why it needs to be kept under constant review.

The Disability Rights Commission was probably the most important body in influencing the content of the Disability Discrimination Act 2004. This legislation introduced a duty on public bodies to proactively take steps to prevent future discrimination. Merely not discriminating was insufficient. In future they needed to look ahead and take measures to prevent discrimination. This provision was not contained in the early anti-discrimination Bills considered by Parliament in the early 1980s. By the time the 2004 Act was passed, everything that had been called for in previous legislation had been achieved and often a great deal more.

But already the Act is showing its age. Had the DRC still been going, I have no doubt it would have resolved the conflict between wheelchair users and people with prams over the use of the accessible space on buses and trains. It could be resolved by simply giving priority in law to wheelchair users. It was impossible to call for such a law even in the early 1990s when the DDA was being drafted, because there were so few accessible spaces that it would have been difficult to justify the parliamentary time.

It is easy to praise the successes in legislative terms that were achieved in the 1980s and 1990s and up to 2010. Much was achieved, but the infrastructure for protecting and building on those achievements was simultaneously being undermined. The creation of the DRC in 2000 resulted in some of the best lobbyist and campaigners in the disability field leaving established charities and joining the staff of the DRC, which was able to offer better terms and conditions and was also the "exciting new kid on the block". Inevitably this weakened the charities from which they came and I noticed the effect this had on my previous employer, RADAR. Also, disabled people who had previously been part of one of the more active groups had also decided to support the DRC, and this meant the new body was strengthened by their presence. The DRC had hoped to leave a legacy of strong organisations led by disabled people and able to take on the DRC's agenda if the new Equality and Human Rights Commission failed to do so. For several reasons, this was not achieved.

From the 1970s through to 2010, campaigning

charities operated under a distinct disadvantage in that charities are forbidden by law from engaging in campaigning which could be seen as party political. As for many years, the Labour Party took a much more positive interest in campaigning for the rights for disabled people than did the Conservative Party, and it was difficult to campaign overtly without appearing to support the Labour point of view. RADAR had always ensured that its researcher for the Parliamentary All Party Disabled Group was strictly politically neutral, and as the officers of the group came from the different parties this was not difficult. However, it would have been inappropriate for any of the major charities to be seen to be publicly criticising one of the political parties on a major aspect of their policy on which they had been elected. This was one of the reasons why many of the larger charities were happy to support and bankroll some of the more radical disability groups but never got involved in party politics.

However, there are times when it is helpful to be more overtly critical of a government policy. During Tony Blair's time as Prime Minister, there was an attempt to alter incapacity benefits. Objections were made unsuccessfully behind the scenes, but one activist group, the Disability Action Network, took themselves to the gates of Downing Street, threw themselves out of their wheelchairs and poured red paint over themselves, illustrating the blood that disabled people were being expected to shed. It produced dramatic pictures for the media and as a result received extensive coverage. I know this one protest was responsible for the government backing down, even though a number of senior Ministers made it clear to Blair that they thought he should hold the line. This could be presented therefore as a major victory, and in the short term it was.

When George Osborne became Chancellor and was determined to cut the Social Security Budget, he introduced a number of changes which have effectively abolished the allowance but also cut many other disability benefits. The disability lobby objected to these changes, but its efforts were unsuccessful. Would it have been better to compromise along the way with the Blair Government and made the benefits less of a target? Or is it better to campaign against negative changes regardless of long-term outcomes which cannot be reasonably predicted? Again, it is a question of lobbying styles.

The major charities had learned to live within the legal restrictions and would not claim to be lobbying the government, merely to be making representations or putting the views of their client group to officials and Ministers etc. Through these relatively simple devices it became possible for the charities to acquire a significant influence in parliamentary circles. It is notable that one of the larger charities, SCOPE, is

withdrawing from providing services for disabled
people, saying it will instead campaign on behalf of
all disabled people, not merely those who have had
cerebral palsy. This will inevitably raise questions
about SCOPE's right to do this and how it can have the
expertise all disability groups would expect it to have.

The economic crash of 2007 had a major impact
on disability charities. Not only did the government
need to rethink its financial priorities but when David
Cameron was elected in 2010 his appointment of
George Osborne as Chancellor had immediate
consequences. Osborne declared openly, during the
election campaign, that he proposed to reduce the size
of the Welfare State. There is no way he could do this
without reducing funding to the NHS, local authorities
and Social Security. These are the big-ticket items
which make up nearly half of Government expenditure.

The cutbacks to local authorities eventually
filtered down to their reducing the support they gave
to disabled people's organisations. Many of these
were small organisations run by disabled people who
campaigned on local disability issues and provided
a valuable stand on the national campaign. As I look
around I see that many of those organisations have
simply disappeared, and others are shadows of their
former selves. Disabled people are still gathering
together and supporting each other in campaigning
and in other ways, but the resources available to

them are miniscule compared to what they once were. One consequence is that disabled people lack the organisational strength to resist many of the current cuts. This could be seen particularly in the cuts to social care services, where the criteria to qualify has been ratcheted up over the years and only those with the most severe disabilities now qualify.

The legislative base has also changed to make it more difficult for charities to campaign. The Transparency of Lobbying, Non-Party Campaigning and Trade Union Administration Act 2014 was originally intended to make commercial lobbying more transparent. Unfortunately, it was changed in Parliament and commercial lobbyists escaped lightly. However it did put heavy restrictions on charities, and particularly those that received funding from the government. For a number of years I served on a small panel funded by the Baring Foundation which looked at the independence of the voluntary sector. Its reports, produced by Civil Exchange, demonstrated that a number of charities had come into direct conflict with the government over campaigning. The government has argued strongly that charities should provide services and should not campaign. This has resulted in a chilling effect on charities, some of which now avoid anything that looks like campaigning and lobbying.

One effect is that the charitable sector is increasingly marginalised by government. This in future will make it difficult for Disability Rights UK to campaign against cuts to social care and healthcare. The disability benefits budget is likely to come under further attack. During the campaign days of the 1990s, one of the slogans used was 'rights not charity'. That is certainly not the view of the current government.

This will have profound obligations for the way in which the disability field operates in future. The campaigning of the past will not be possible unless the Lobbying Act is radically amended or abolished. Major charities will be more circumspect in how to present their arguments. This will lead to an opening for small informal groups that do not have charitable status to lead some of the major political battles. This is already being reflected in some aspects of politics, with new groups appearing suddenly and growing quickly. But most small disability groups are poorly funded and their members have higher mobility costs and other costs. Back in the 1970s the Disablement Income Group did its campaigning through a separate trust, and the larger charities might need to consider similar tactics today. It is also possible to see opportunities for larger charities to work with small activist groups to support future campaigns. Of one thing I am certain – it will be difficult in future for charities to campaign as they did before 2010.

It will also be difficult for charities to influence policy through quangos. This is largely because so many have been abolished, and those that remain have had their budgets reduced and their wings clipped. In short, there is no evidence that the government values external advice, and this does not augur well for the future.

I believe that in future the biggest danger to support for disabled people will be in those areas of public provision which are under great pressure. If the current Government remains in power, privatisation of the Health Service seems to me to some extent inevitable. The major cutbacks will be in behind-the-scenes support. Increasingly, social care will be seen as removing people from hospital beds. As health and social care become increasingly linked there will be a diminution of the social care services built up in recent decades.

Disabled people will need to develop mechanisms to either defend current systems or create new ones.

Many of the major structural changes achieved in recent decades are probably sufficiently embedded to survive. This will include access to education, support for employment services, access to buildings and public transport *et cetera*. However, these could be weakened, as has happened in the case of housing, where access standards were made discretionary unless local authorities decided to enforce them. This can be made easier for the government by the Bill which at the time of writing was before Parliament on

Brexit. Allowing the government of the day to amend current European law and regulation without reference to Parliament enables a great deal of good legislation to be weakened or repealed on the basis of reducing red tape. This represents one of the major threats in the future.

On the positive side, the lives and profile disabled people enjoy today are so much better than in the 1960s. Personal mobility is much improved too, although the implications of driverless and electric vehicles will need watching. I'm not sure the public would accept public transport reverting to the standards of the 1970s. I feel most of the gains are here to stay. This argument can be developed further, but the outcome of the work over the last 50 years has been positive. I recall in the mid-1980s sitting on a committee with Richard Attenborough to promote greater participation of disabled people in the arts. At that time it was impossible to envisage the large number of disabled people who regularly appear in the media dealing with issues that are not disability based.

Disabled people have arrived. We need to ensure that the high profile we have achieved does not mask how much remains to be done.

Chapter 12
No Such Thing As Retirement

by Bob Niven and Ann Frye

This Chapter focuses on Sir Bert and his work in his last ten years. Bert was not able to write it before he died, so he asked us, as former colleagues and friends, to do so. It is therefore inevitably an account "from the outside", although we are most grateful to the many people who worked with him during this period and generously gave us their recollections and impressions.[35]

---

35. In particular Alan Bornat, David Cutler, Stella Coulthurst, Brian Donnelly, Steve Hawkins, Rod Hill, Andrew Holroyd and the late Richard Sermon.

Bert's final decade saw him spending most of his time in Liverpool, in a very happy marriage with Lady Maureen. He continued to keep in close touch with the extended family, taking some holidays and reading avidly, especially about history. However he also remained remarkably active to the end in helping to lead and support organisations and initiatives concerned with disability and disadvantage – nationally and locally, above all in and around Merseyside. After his death in October 2017, it was striking and symbolic that the two memorial events to celebrate his life attracted hundreds of people; they were held in the Houses of Parliament and in the Reds Lounge at Anfield, Liverpool Football Club.

The decade from 2008 saw a number of continuities from earlier years, in addition to his years with the Equality and Human Rights Commission. In 2003 Bert became and remained to the end a Patron of the Heswall Disabled Children's Holiday Fund, the same fund that had enabled him to enjoy fun and adventures in his teens (Chapter 3). He sustained his long-standing active involvement in and support for Habinteg, promoting inclusive and accessible housing for disabled people. From 2004 he was Vice President of the Muscular Dystrophy Campaign, and he maintained close links with the Independent Living Foundation, the Polio Fellowship and Mobility Choice.

Bert continued as a member of the Worshipful Company of Wheelwrights. He was able to provide advice to the Company, which through its charitable activities and more generally places a special emphasis on practical support for disabled people. He had received the Master Wheelwright's Award in 2001, and in 2018 the Company announced it was introducing the Sir Bert Massie medal to be awarded annually to people who had made a special contribution to improving the lives of disabled people.

Independent mobility was always one of Bert's top priorities, both for himself and for other disabled people. Over the years, his own vehicles became ever more sophisticated and able to accommodate his need for increasing levels of assistance both in getting in and out and in controlling the vehicle. His last vehicle enabled him to drive in comfort out of a wheelchair – a long way from the days of the "Noddy car" with which he started his lifetime of independent travel.

For others, Bert's continuing passion to ensure accessible transport was foreshadowed by his remark at RADAR in the 1990s: "By 2012 every taxi will be wheelchair accessible. Now we at the Royal Association for Disability and Rehabilitation need to work on boats and aeroplanes. Eventually we will have to work on space travel, because the minute there are trips to space there will be some doctor saying this is bad for your health and disabled people cannot do it.

We'll be there saying 'No, sunshine. If you can go into space, we are going as well.' We do have rights. We are full members of society."

In 2011 Bert wrote that it was worth recalling just how much progress had been made on transport. He said it was an impressive journey, although new pressures had grown around the world affecting how all of us travel. He judged that the effects of measures such as security and a never-ending quest to reduce costs had a disproportionately adverse impact on disabled people and that some of the successes of the past were in danger of being destroyed.

The task was ongoing. Bert would recall that at an airport in Egypt he was being loaded onto a lift-in platform when the mechanism failed. He was there for some time, about four metres above the ground. Bert commented: "The novel way to resolve this, or so I was told, was that I should fall out of my wheelchair toward the ground and the staff would catch me. While I can do nothing other than applaud their enthusiasm, I am afraid my faith in their ability was not so strong that I was prepared to do this, and we had to find another method!"

More generally, new developments required continuing vigilance. He wrote: "It would I think be extremely unfortunate if we allowed the cyber world to become as inaccessible as the physical world once was, especially as so much interaction takes place within the cyber world."

In 2002, Bert took on a role as a Governor of Motability, the body that supplies cars, scooters and wheelchairs to severely disabled people in exchange for their Disability Living Allowance (formerly Mobility Allowance). This was a role to which Bert gave a great deal of time and energy right up to his final few months.

Although a great supporter of the scheme, Bert was always ready to hold the organisation to account and to challenge any aspect or proposal that he saw as not being in the best interests of disabled people. Through the Scheme Oversight Committee on which he served, he was much involved in monitoring the customer service levels, value for money, affordability and reliability of the service. He could be a fierce critic both of the organisation as a whole and of any proposed initiative that he saw as deflecting attention from the core purpose of Motability.

The Motability chairman, Lord Sterling, relied heavily on Bert as a sounding board and would regularly phone him for advice or to try out a new idea. Unfortunately, Lord Sterling's preferred time of calling on a Sunday morning would often coincide with Bert's preferred time for a leisurely bath!

Bert also wrote detailed and closely-argued letters to Lord Sterling and others with an often forensic analysis of why the latest Government proposal would not work. In one such letter he commented tersely: "Once again we are being asked to ignore all the principles on which the Motability scheme has been based since its origin." Indeed, Bert was concerned that the government seemed increasingly to forget the fact that Motability was an independent charity over which it had no authority.

He also had concerns about the financial arrangements of the Motability scheme, and in particular the policy on reserves, which has since emerged as a highly contentious issue. Writing in 2016, Bert commented: "Motability could serve its current customers better, promote research into other ways of supporting a wider range of disabled people and play a greater partnership role with appropriate charities and other organisations. This would not only be an effective use of our funds but would also be a public demonstration of Motability using its funds wisely and creatively."

Bert's role in Motability is another clear example of his unerring moral compass and his refusal to compromise on what he believed were the best interests of disabled people.

Bert also took on a wide range of new roles and responsibilities. At national level, in 2008 Bert was appointed Commissioner for the Compact. First established in 1998, the Compact was an agreement between government and the voluntary and community sector to "improve their relationship for mutual advantage and community gain". Over time, its application was widened to cover the wider third sector as well as non-departmental government bodies and local authorities. The Compact focused on service delivery, partnership-building and encouraging innovation. Its many outputs included a wide range of publications with advice and good practice as well as conferences and seminars, on such issues as funding and grant-making, leadership and management, policy formation and procurement of services, consultation and community involvement. Bert was active both as an ambassador for the Compact and within the organisation. His interest in and care for staff was a further hallmark, at the Compact and the other organisations in which he was involved.

There was general acceptance that the Compact was "a good thing", but it struggled to be fully effective. It had a vast remit, and it was difficult to secure active involvement from all parts of the public and third sectors. In particular, the Compact lacked a statutory basis and Bert worked hard to secure this. He nearly succeeded, but in the end the government did not introduce legislation. This was a blow to Bert. The Compact continued to decline and was in effect wound up by the then Coalition Government in 2011.

However, he sustained his support for the third sector, including joining the Baring Foundation Panel on the Independence of the Voluntary Sector. He also chaired the Volunteer Centre in Liverpool, which provides a one-stop resource for information, advice and guidance on all aspects of volunteering for potential volunteers as well as voluntary and community organisations. The Centre also provides accredited training and qualifications for volunteers.

Throughout his career, Bert had championed the rights and needs of the disadvantaged and had been a (not uncritical) supporter of the Labour Party. For example, as early as 1993 he had been one of the sixteen distinguished members of the wide-ranging Commission on Social Justice, established by the Institute for Public Policy and Research and a major influence on the thinking of the Party at the time. Bert led on the Commission's publication "Disability and Social Justice". Twenty years later he chaired the Independent Taskforce on Disability and Poverty and submitted to the Party its report on "Breaking the Link between Disability and Poverty".

As described elsewhere in this book, Bert had also served on a wide range of statutory and other public influential committees and task forces. He was very widely respected as a skilful and successful wielder of influence and persuasion. An article of his published in 2010 described his approach.[36] His advice included: ensure you are working from facts and not just emotion; understand, but above all respect, the views of those you are opposing before you try to

36. "Changemakers on Campaigning and Influencing Skills for Effective Engagement", Sir Bert Massie, in Meet the Change-makers:, Expert Tips for Effective Engagement, Association of Chief Executives of Voluntary Organisations (ACEVO) 2010

alter their beliefs; put the work in – campaigning and influencing are about the long haul; be persistent; tailor your messages and keep them simple; don't be afraid to have your opinions changed; focus on what can be done; and maintain your integrity – be principled to win. Many others would also emphasise Bert's use of humour and his inclusiveness.

Bert joined the boards of several organisations concerned with disability and the rights of other disadvantaged groups. In 2012, together with its Chief Executive, Brian Donnelly, Bert helped to establish CECOPS, a Community Interest Company concerned to ensure standards and certification for assistive technologies of all kinds for disabled people (including for home living and nursing, wheelchairs, communications and telecare). Bert remained CECOPS' Chair until his death, when Mr. Donnelly wrote that Bert had been a champion for the cause and that CECOPS' growth was largely due to his wisdom, experience and passion.

Sir Bert was invited to be a Trustee at Local Solutions, which is concerned with the disadvantaged, excluded and vulnerable in Liverpool and parts of North Wales. Local Solutions' extensive initiatives and programmes address among other things accommodation for young people and families, employability, welfare advice and guidance, anti-bullying, and support for unpaid carers as well as victims of domestic abuse. The Chief Executive told us of Bert's huge commitment to the issues as well as his helpful advice to him on governance and key management issues. Soon after Bert died, Local Solutions launched its "Wheely Boat", a cruising launch berthed in Liverpool, designed especially for wheelchair users and named in Bert's honour.

Bert also served on the Board of RAISE, an independent charity centred on Merseyside and Runcorn. RAISE gives confidential advice to individuals on welfare benefits, addressing debt and money management issues. Board colleagues recall Bert's commitment to the people helped by RAISE (including housing association tenants) and his consistently valuable advice on governance and related issues faced by the then relatively small and new organisation (it is now highly effective). They also recall, as do many others with whom Bert worked, his ability to challenge constructively as well as his telling of jokes (sometimes idiosyncratic).

Bert continued his lifelong attachment to, and interest, in Liverpool and Merseyside. In 2014 this culminated in his being commissioned as a Deputy Lieutenant of Merseyside by the Lord Lieutenant.

Bert had previously been involved with international disability bodies including the European Disability Forum, the European Polio Fellowship and Rehabilitation International. During the period covered by this chapter he was also active in Liverpool on behalf of Rights and Humanity, the international organisation concerned with human rights as the basis of economic development and ending conflicts.

The provision of care for disabled and older people had always been a key concern of Bert's. In a new departure, he joined the Board of Appleshaw Group Ltd as a non-executive director. Appleshaw had been established to develop and operate privately-financed continuing-care retirement communities. These were intended to bring together all aspects of older care in a high-quality self-sufficient community and were designed around the needs and wishes of older people, including the provision of, but not limited to, individual independent living homes, nursing services (for frailty and dementia) and personal care. Bert was a valued and active member of the Board, which also comprised leading figures from the health service, business and the world of finance - Bert used to joke that he risked being turned into a capitalist. In 2008 Appleshaw had clinched its first proposed development when the financial crash led to its sources of financial backing drying up. But by 2017 a very similar proposal, based exactly on the principles and practicalities Bert had helped to fashion, was being taken forward.

Bert also established his own disability consultancy business, which included assisting a leading organisation in Dubai to improve the circumstances of disabled people there. Other activities included giving speeches, chairing conferences and editing publications; whether he charged a fee or not depended on the resources of the organisation in question.

Bert took great pride and pleasure in his numerous appointments and roles. In the academic world, in addition to his Doctorate of Laws awarded by the University of Bristol in 2005, Staffordshire University in 2007 conferred on him the Honorary Award of Doctor of the University for outstanding services to promoting the rights of disabled people. In 2009 he was awarded a Fellowship to the City and Guilds of London in recognition of his outstanding professional and personal achievements, and in 2013 he received the Degree of Doctor of Laws from Liverpool University.

No appointment gave him greater pleasure than when in 2008 he was appointed an independent member of the Board of Governors of Liverpool John Moores University. As mentioned in earlier chapters, he graduated from the then Liverpool Polytechnic in 1977and in 2002 had been awarded an Honorary Fellowship by the University.

He carried out a number of formal roles as Governor, serving as Chair of the Audit Committee and a member of the Remuneration and Nominations Committee as well as the Chairs Group. He also took a keen interest in diversity issues: he for example played a leading role in the University's large-scale events on equalities, diversity and human rights as well as on the future of the Equality Act and the event "Keeping Race Equality on the Agenda". He was an active Governor and visible to the students. The Chair of the Governors greatly appreciated his keen interest in the University, his constructive challenges as a Board member and his ability to help the Chair manage Board business efficiently and successfully even on difficult issues.

On Bert's death, the University published a tribute (the spirit of which reflects the many other tributes at the time). The University wrote: "Sir Bert was a wonderful member of our extended family, and a great ambassador for the University. A dedicated member of our Governing Body, he took his role as a critical friend seriously, he spoke eloquently on behalf of our students and our staff and was a true role model to so many of us. He will be remembered fondly for his immense contribution… and for his genuine interest… He will be sadly missed". And at the memorial event held at Anfield in June 2018, the University very generously announced an annual bursary worth £10,000 for a student sharing Sir Bert's values.

Postscript

Bert's cancer took hold during 2016 but, greatly helped by Lady Maureen, he continued to be very active, including writing most of this book and in terms of meetings, engagements and a holiday in Spain. From mid-July 2017 hospital appointments and radiotherapy became increasingly frequent. During his last few days in October, he sought to speak by phone to close friends and colleagues. Despite travel difficulties, some 200 people attended his funeral in Liverpool.

We have not sought to amend or add to the chapters which Bert wrote and which make up the great bulk of this book, even though we know that they do not mention all that he did or all those he worked with. However the book has hopefully captured the essence of the man as well as the huge range of his activities and achievements at all levels as an activist, advocate, policy adviser, writer, thinker, leader and inspirer of others.

His record is unequalled on improving the lives of disabled people in the United Kingdom, and it is no exaggeration to say that Bert was one of the leading social reformers since World War II. Not bad for a severely disabled person brought up in working-class Liverpool who nearly died from polio at three months old.

Ann Frye
Bob Niven